MAN IN THE OLD TESTAMENT

STUDIES IN BIBLICAL THEOLOGY · 4

MAN IN THE OLD TESTAMENT

WALTHER EICHRODT

Translated by

K. *and* R. GREGOR SMITH

SCM PRESS LTD
BLOOMSBURY STREET LONDON

The English version of
DAS MENSCHENVERSTÄNDNIS
DES ALTEN TESTAMENTS
(Zwingli-Verlag Zürich)

334 00956 1

First published 1951
by SCM Press Ltd
56 Bloomsbury Street London WC1
Second impression 1954
Third impression 1956
Fourth impression 1959
Fifth impression 1961
Sixth impression 1966
Seventh impression 1970

Printed in Great Britain by
Lewis Reprints Limited, Port Talbot, Glamorgan

CONTENTS

INTRODUCTION

THE question how we are to understand human life is being asked among us to-day with a new intensity. In the tumult of our present existence the human spirit is seeking new and better ways of understanding its place and task in our time. This is only possible if one wrestles with those interpretations of the enigma of man which are among the basic factors of the contemporary spiritual situation. Among these interpretations the Old Testament view of man (of which the Christian view of life sees itself as the fulfilment) demands the special attention of every investigator, even if only on account of the breadth and depth of its influence, on Judaism and Islam as well as on Christianity. The Old Testament view of man is also supremely important for everyone concerned with the question of God, since it offers an interpretation of life which is almost unique in that it proceeds from a constant relation with the will of God as revealed in the Word, and answers the question of man in the light of the redemption it perceives there. At the same time this Old Testament view is tested and confirmed in the whole complex of human relationships, in family, kindred, people, state and the world of nations. The Christian in particular must recognize that he can properly grasp the New Testament view of man, and successfully protect it from misunderstanding, only if he knows the Old Testament interpretation of life.

7

It is true that the task of representing the Old Testament view of man is fraught with various difficulties. First, the question will be raised whether it is possible to speak at all of an Old Testament view of man without doing violence to the rich historical variety of the Old Testament witnesses; whether one ought not rather to speak of different types of Old Testament understanding of life, of the prophetic and the priestly (to name only the chief), or of the ancient Israelite and the Jewish types. Such doubts certainly have their place. But if it is right to say that despite all its historical complexity the Old Testament does give the impression of religious unity, then in considering the common material which undeniably binds together the different historical expressions of the Old Testament message, we are justified, not indeed in passing over the particular, but in paying primary attention to the spiritual unity which is present even in the differences.

There is a second difficulty—the extent of the material to be surveyed. If the presentation is not to be unduly swollen there must be a certain selection from the wealth of detail. One may thereby lay oneself open to the reproach of having overlooked this or that. My argument does not depend on completeness in every detail. My attempt in what follows has been rather to sketch the main outlines of the Old Testament interpretation of the enigma of man, in the hope that my readers may be stimulated to come to grips themselves with this rich theme.

CHAPTER ONE

THE UNCONDITIONAL OBLIGATION OF THE WILL OF GOD AS THE BASIS OF THE OLD TESTAMENT VIEW OF MAN

1. *Its peculiar form and development in the Law*

T H E basic phenomenon peculiar to man is the consciousness ✳ of responsibility. In primitive man this is chiefly expressed as collective responsibility, in which the consciousness of the I remains uncertain and weakly developed. Only when responsibility breaks through the collective constraint and releases the individual from his circle, making him rely on himself as a responsible individual, is it possible for full personal consciousness to awaken. This takes place among ancient civilizations with especial clarity in the legal constitution. Traces of the old primitive conception of guilt may still be perceived, by which the wrongdoer, in conscious or unconscious violation of objective norms, is expelled to a magic world of curses—it does not matter whether he is conscious of guilt or not—and his immediate circle, his family and kindred, are also drawn into the realm of the curse. This external constraint of objective guilt with its collective implication is, however, increasingly superseded. The subjective responsibility of the individual becomes established as decisive in the attribution of guilt. The newly awakened recognition of individual life as independent and valuable makes its influence clearly felt. The significance of this event in the forming of the person may be traced even in Babylonian and Assyrian law. But it is in Greece that the proud consciousness of the free citizen stands in the closest connexion with that responsibility towards the *nomos* of the community which is shared by all, yet lays its demands on each individual as such. This basic conviction is asserted in the Law of ancient Israel with peculiar force and consistency. The Book of the Covenant, Ex. 20-23, which goes back at least to the time of entry into the promised land, and codifies still earlier customs, gives us a valuable insight into the relation between the protection afforded by the Law to the community as a whole, and the claim made on the Law by the individual. It is a very illuminating fact that collective retribution as a principle of punishment has ceased to play any part in this code. It is true that in the carrying out of legal retribution the idea of solidarity of guilt is still effective, in that the individual's transgression is also avenged on his immediate family circle or kindred, whether in cases of treachery or of primitive belief in a curse which demands extraordinary means of expiation, as when the sons of Saul were delivered up to the vengeance of the Canaanite city of Gibeon (II Sam. 21). But in the code the individual wrongdoer is consistently made responsible in his own person, while his family is not touched. As the 'Thou shalt' of the categorical command is directed at the individual Israelite, whether male or female, full citizen or sojourner in Israel, so the punishment of the Law is executed only on the guilty person, his kin not even being incriminated in those cases where the ancient Eastern conception of justice (as is borne out by Babylonian and Assyrian laws) unhesitatingly includes them, for example in cases of indirect talion.[1] And since in the assessment of the individual's guilt questions are asked about his

---

[1] These are concerned with the punishment of the nearest kinsman of the convicted man, especially when the offence is traced to indirect guilt, e.g. in housebreaking as a consequence of faulty work by the architect. Cf. in the Code of Hammurabi, §229-30, and the similar cases in §116 and 210, in Wilhelm Eilers, *Die Gesetzesstele Chammurabis*, 1932 (Der alte Orient, 31, 3/4). For the Assyrian law cf. H. Eheloff, *Ein altassyrisches Rechtsbuch übersetzt*, 49, p. 41f. (Mitteilungen aus der Vorderasiatischen Abteilung der Staatlichen Museen zu Berlin, 1, 1922).

knowledge and intention[2] he is not only considered to be a subject at law in regard to the carrying out of his deed, but he is also considered as a moral subject who is responsible for the inner reasons for his action. Guilt, from being an objective fate which drags the doer with it, irrespective of his inner relation to his deed, becomes a matter of personal and conscious responsibility.

This breaking down of the collective way of thinking which dominated primitive peoples, with its idea of objective guilt having the character of a taboo, affects not only the calculation of guilt but also the establishment of punishment. When, in sharp contrast to the custom of other peoples, capital punishment ceases to be inflicted in Israel for crimes against property, this has nothing to do with a general relaxation of the ancient strict calculation of punishment as we may observe it, for instance among the Hittites,[3] since in other cases this most severe punishment of all is still enforced. It is rather that the personal thought of ancient Israel as a community of justice is illuminated from a new angle: in contrast to all value attached to things the life of the guilty man is reckoned as unconditionally more valuable, so that it cannot be balanced against the damage done, and may not be sacrificed to the egoistic protection of property by the community.

This moral personalism in the Law is emphasized from yet a third side, in the law regarding slaves. Not only is the punishment of mutilation, by the cutting off of nose, ears, or the like, abolished, but legal protection is also given to the life of the slave over against his own master. The master pays for serious harm occasioned by bodily maltreatment, by having to

---

[2] Cf., e.g., the conditions in the law regarding the goring ox, Ex. 21.29, 36.

[3] Cf. J. Friedrich and H. Zimmern, *Hethitische Gesetze aus dem Staatsarchiv von Boghazköi* (Der alte Orient, 23, 2, 1922). Here capital punishment is actually abolished for murder (I.1ff.), while it is still enforced in the case of the theft of a sacred object from the royal palace (II.23).

set the slave free, and the murder of the slave is also punished.[4] If we compare with this the almost unlimited power of the owner over his slave throughout the ancient world, then we may trace this encroachment on an otherwise unquestioned privilege to the power of the idea of the person, a power opposed even in the Israel of early times to the traditional collective relationships.

The Law provides us also with a complete proof that in the later historical epochs Israel retained its sense as a people for the unconditional personal value of man, and even understood it better and gave it deeper foundations; and this in spite of the change from monarchy to despotism, in spite of the proletariatization of the lower classes, in spite of the humiliation of rule by foreigners. The Book of the Law, which three decades before the downfall of the State had shown the way to an audacious attempt at thorough reform, and exerted absolute authority on all succeeding generations, the Book of Deuteronomy, shows by the remarkable form in which it proclaims the Law how little it expected of justice imposed by force. With passionate seriousness this book pleads with the people for their inner acceptance of the new structure loyally raised on the foundations of the old popular Law. The appeal to the heart and conscience of his hearers shows that the law-giver looked on the awakening of a completely personal sense of responsibility as the basic presupposition of a healthy Law. And in speaking of love of God as the tap-root of all loyalty to the Law, and expressing this love in the form 'Thou shalt' as the basic demand of the divine Lawgiver,[5] he summons the highest strength of the moral life of the person to the aid of the whole.

Even the code whose main contents are the basic ordinances of the cult, the code which seems to be devoted to the proper functioning of the machinery of the cult, that is, the priestly law

---

[4] Ex. 21.20f., 26f   [5] Deut. 6.5.

in the Book of Leviticus, is perfectly aware of the fundamental importance of individual decision. Its all-embracing norm for the Law is the thought of love, and with the sentence, 'Thou shalt love thy neighbour as thyself', the misuse of the code as a rigid limitation of social relationships is avoided.[6] In this way it appeals to the much higher power of moral life, which lifts all legal relationships out of the realm of a struggle for power and egoistic self-preservation and fills them with its spirit. But when the Law points beyond itself in this way, opposing all external legalism with the personal effort of the individual, it must be able to reach down into a living awareness in the people of the personal responsibility of each member, an awareness which is irreconcilably opposed to all collectivism.

In view of these facts about the Law of Israel it may be affirmed without exaggeration that in no other people of the ancient East is the sense of the responsibility of each member of the people so living, and the personal attitude so dominant. The explanation lies in the religious basis of the Law of Israel.

2. *The intensity of the consciousness of obligation as a result of its religious basis*

(*a*) Among Israel's neighbours, too, it is not arbitrary human choice, but transcendent divine authority, which summons man to responsibility. This is what links the dignity of the individual with the sphere of holiness. As the Babylonian or Assyrian king substantiates his position as ruler by claiming that it is a call from one of the chief gods, he is also concerned to proclaim a god as being the author and guarantor of the legal system he upholds. Hammurabi derives his code from the command of the sun-god Shamash, the great judge of heaven and

[6] Lev. 19.18, 34.

earth, and invokes all the gods to protect the new order. And the Greeks see in the laws of their State the divine law, maintained by Diké, the partner of Zeus, and defended and avenged by the gods. Thus man sees himself as a member of a divine order.

This religious basis to legal obligation, however, was not able to instil into man the sense of unconditioned responsibility. For among the civilized peoples of the ancient East the guarantee of the holiness of the law was provided by a variety of nature-gods. Since the plans of these gods often contradicted one another, individual life was safeguarded by means of magic arts, and it was always possible to withdraw from the threat of their wrath to the cover of the sacrificial cults. In this situation it is therefore never possible for the unique significance of moral obligation to be developed: the naturalism in the conception of the gods is bound to have a stifling effect. In addition, there is the irresistible secularization of the concept of law. The king's code develops out of the divine order without the possibility of any serious resistance from the gods. Hammurabi emphatically defines his code as 'the law of the land which I have given, the decisions of the land which I have made'. And the deification of the king greatly facilitates the prominent position given to the human lawgiver. Thus the interpretation of individual life, apart from several new beginnings in the wisdom teaching, remains on the whole on a vitalist-eudaemonistic basis: life is bound up with the longing for good-fortune and the fear of ill-fortune.

In Greece, on the other hand, the gods are so closely bound up with the state that their transcendent will imperceptibly withdraws behind the sovereignty of the citizens over the law. As a further consequence, with the fall of the *polis* an end is also made to divine authority as the basis of justice. This necessitates a re-establishment of the law, which in spite of its religious spirit pursues an essentially rational course, replacing religion by science (*Wissenschaft*). Human law is given its assured place within this total view of the world as an ordered and regular unity. From this new starting-point a view of man's individual life is obtained which is not derived from the basic datum of human obligation and responsibility, but interprets man's being on the basis of a view of the cosmos as a unity, understanding him as an ordered microcosm with its laws on the analogy of the macrocosm.

In Israel the religious basis of human responsibility presents us with a quite different picture. From the beginning it is filled with an inner strength and an exclusive power for which in the whole of the ancient world we have a remote analogy perhaps only in Zarathustra. For the divine authority behind the Law has nothing to do with a world of many gods with as many minds. Nor has it to do with a general sphere of the numinous, with the oppressive constraint of some unexplained taboo. But this divine authority is concentrated in a single personal will, which takes complete hold of the man addressed by it, and tolerates no other claim. Here the obligation imposed by the Law is unconditional, and cannot be avoided by recourse to any other divine court of appeal more kindly disposed to human interests, like the personal tutelary gods of paganism. Nor can it be avoided by magical practices or exorcisms which compel the desired result. In the strict 'Thou shalt' of the Decalogue and of other brief basic laws it is not some human lawgiver but the divine Lawgiver himself who speaks and makes his will the absolute norm.

It is true that this 'Thou shalt' originates not in civil life but in the cultic ritual of the people, that is, the place where the voice of the divine Lord of the Covenant is heard in the man commissioned by him, summoning his people to respond.[7] What is unique and without any analogy, however, is that the 'Thou shalt' invades secular civil law, which is very different

---

[7] Cf. the portrayal in Deut. 27, and A. Alt, *Die Ursprünge des Israelitischen Rechts*, 1934, p. 59ff.

in character, and again and again breaks through its deliberate legal style, and its many conditional clauses, with its categorical command. This can be seen happening in the Book of the Covenant.[8] This means that a form of law which had originated on other soil (that of the legal tradition rising out of the normal judgements of the local courts in the villages and towns, handed down with substantial unanimity throughout the Near East) was made subject to the unconditional claim of the God of Sinai as the Lord who recognized no secular or neutral zone. Apodeictic demands, aflame with the will of the jealous God, disclose an aggressive force which transforms the ancient Eastern law from its more or less neutral attitude to religion, giving its distinctive character to the whole history of the development of the Law in Israel.[9] Thus not only the Law of the cult but also the civil Law acquires the character of a direct demand of God. Transgression of the Law is not only rebellion against the civil community, but also an outrage against God himself.

(b) This unconditioned obligation, beneath which individual life is thus placed, receives its unique quality through entering into the closest connexion with the consciousness of Israel as a people. Israel was never able to regard its growth into a nation as a simple natural fact, but saw it as an undeserved gift of God, who had freed it from its helot existence in Egypt and made possible its growth into a powerful and self-conscious people by binding it together with a common Law and giving it possession of a free homeland. From then on Israel knew itself to be the special people of this God who had bound it inseparably with himself by means of a Covenant. It was shown that the great task of its existence, and the fulfilment of its meaning, lay in the worship of God and in the realization of a national order pleasing to him. This meant that the divine demand, which was laid with such exclusive power on the in-

---

[8] Ex. 21.12-17; 22.17, 20f., 27; 23.1-3, 6-9.
[9] See p. 12f.

dividual, was from the beginning embedded in a *history* of this God with his people. In this history the divine Lawgiver was recognized from the beginning as the divine Lifegiver, and his demand was distinguished from all arbitrary tyranny as a call to a relation of grace. And the individual's obligation, in the 'Thou shalt' of the Law, received from this relation of grace an inner motivation and illumination in virtue of which it was seen, not as a heavy yoke, but as a necessary and blessed form of life, as a liberation from chaotic self-destruction.

This is what lies behind the enthusiasm of devotion and sacrificial service which we see breaking forth again and again in ancient Israel, when the sacred Covenant summoned it to common action.[10] That man lives by God's Law is the conviction already present here, though unexpressed, and later to be so strongly emphasized in the Deuteronomic code and in Ezekiel.[11]

(*c*) These peculiar conditions of Israel's conception of the Law of God were to be attacked from different sides in the course of Israel's history. In particular, Israel's view was threatened by the same danger of a gradual infusion into the Law of worldliness and secularization as may be observed in the great civilizations of the ancient world. The consciousness of direct divine guidance and of the obligation of the whole people was weakened especially by the transformation of the nation's external life from that of a sacred covenantal society into a territorial state, which united Canaanites, who had their own cultural tradition, with the tribes of Israel. Just as the leadership of the host in war no longer required the charismatists, whose abrupt and incalculable rise out of obscurity to the front rank of the people had been the most palpable sign of the divine call and leadership, but was taken over by the king and

---

[10] For a most powerful expression of this, see the Song of Deborah, Judg. 5, which belongs to the earliest period of entry into the promised land.

[11] Deut. 4.1, 8, 40; 5.30, etc.; Ezek. 20.11, 13, 21.

B

his professional soldiers and practised in accordance with the customary rules of war, in the same way there was an impulse in every sphere to rationalization and accommodation to the tested rules of civilization, rules which elevated to unprecedented importance the standpoint of what was practicable and what offered security for the enjoyment of life. The *élan* and audacity of a level of life with still unexhausted possibilities, was lost more and more in a narrow and calculating round of existence. And the more this happened, the more inevitable was the threatened decline, if not total extinction, of the sense of a direct relation between God and the whole people, as well as between God and individuals.

In the realm of the Law this could only have led to the break-up of the living unity of cultic and social Law, to the withdrawal of the Deity as the real Lawgiver behind human authorities, and to the replacement of the religious orientation of the Law by a moralistic and legalistic conception. We are sufficiently acquainted with these phenomena in Babylonian and Assyrian law. But for Israel the decisive factor is that in the development of the Law, as in its first formation, reliance on the divine Lawgiver was maintained. In consequence, all tendencies to secularization were opposed. In opposition to the monarchy, the most prominent example of these tendencies, the claim of the divine personal will to give the decisive shape to Israel's life was again and again successfully asserted. It is true that a new royal law was inserted into the structure of the Law, which gave the practice of a part of the law into the hands of the king, whose decision then affected, with the authority of a supreme court of appeal, the decisions of the elders in the local courts. But when the monarchy attempted to extend its power in disregard of the ancient holy Law of God, it met with un-yielding opposition. From the time of Saul's disregard of the ancient law of the ban, in his triumphal ceremony after the campaign against the Amalekites, and his refusal to render absolute obedience to God's demand, following instead what was humanly expedient,[12] there is no end to the attempts to make the monarchy an exception to the duty of absolute obedience to the divine ordinance. Opposed as they were to the unscrupulous extension of royal power, the restrictions of the divinely sanctioned popular laws appeared, to the politically successful ruler in particular, to be an intolerable limitation upon a necessary development, which everywhere else was regarded as a matter of course. Thus the outwardly brilliant rule of the house of Omri, which marked a climax in the political development of North Israel, brought with it an influx of Canaanite-Phoenician royal law, as well as an assimilation of religion, from motives of political expediency, to the surrounding world, and a brutal suppression of the free Law of the people.[13] And the period of Assyrian rule under kings like Manasseh and Ahaz saw the triumph of Assyrian justice in the Jewish state.[14]

However deep the wounds inflicted by these events on the genuinely Israelite conception of the Law, they were not serious enough to win any lasting victory over the sense of unconditioned obligation to the demand of God. The foreign body was thrown out again, sometimes to the accompaniment of severe inner crises, and the living spark of the Law kindled to a bright flame. Thus the people not only continued to co-operate in important acts of state, as may be seen, for example, in the Josianic reform, shortly before the end of the Jewish national state,[15] but the king's position as servant of the Most High, responsible to his will, was upheld against all attempts at his deification. The uncompromising struggle for the right line between the king's and the people's Law is seen both in the prophetic accounts of the Books of Kings and in the remarkable document of the so-called royal code in Deuteronomy.[16] This limitation on a condition of affairs which was taken for granted

[12] I Sam. 15.
[13] II Kings 17f.; 21.
[14] Isa. 10.1ff.; II Kings 16.10ff.; 21.1ff., 16.

[15] II Kings 22f.
[16] Deut. 17.14-20.

in all oriental States points to a strength in the Israelite sense of the Law, which can be explained only in terms of the belief in God which bound together as 'brothers' all members of the people. But it was still more important that in the new collections of laws which were made at the end of the monarchical period, in Deuteronomy and the priestly law, the claim of the personal divine will was given still sharper and more unequivocal expression. These books taught that the divine love or the divine holiness was to be understood as the motivating force of the divine being; they expounded the final purpose of the Law as consisting in the direct relation of the whole life with the divine Thou; and they thereby provided both the cultic and the politico-social orders with their inner unity as the guide to the proper human response to the divine summons.[17]

3. *The deepening of the direct relation with God in prophecy and its effects*

This peculiar development of the Law, with its continual return from all extension and ramification in casuistry to the final metaphysical basis of all Law, is, however, only one part of the great spiritual movement which gives the history of Israel the character of a struggle for direct relation with God. The most powerful expression of this struggle is undoubtedly to be found in the prophets. Here is to be seen the most resolute defence against all those social movements in religion which are reared like isolating walls around the individual, robbing him of the sense of being set face to face with God, and forcing him down into the mass. The terrible attack on the monarchy, in which the nation was seeking its religious illumination, the attack against the priesthood, which with its colossal mass dis-

[17] For the development of the Law of Israel cf. my *Theologie des Alten Testaments*, I, 36ff.

play of cultic achievements offered itself as the sure guarantee
of God's grace, the attack against professional prophecy, which
had stiffened into a guild which was the ready servant of both
king and priest—these attacks were simultaneously the advocacy
of the unconditioned lordship of Yahweh and the unconditioned
support of a direct relation between God and the individual
which gave the individual his personal dignity. The cry *shubu*
—'Turn!'—sounds through this whole period as one of the
basic words of the prophetic proclamation, and this asks of
the individual a conscious decision against the constraint of the
collective will and against the pressure of a cultural development
encouraged by the whole external situation. In the struggle
against the reduction of religion to a mass affair by means of a
refined exercise of the cult, the watch-cry was coined, 'Not
sacrifice, but obedience!'[18] and here again the individual is
torn from his comfortable position in the religious life of the
community and summoned to use his own judgement and make
his own decisive contribution. Most remarkable in this connexion are the new form and forceful concentration of the
relation with God, which had hitherto simply been described as
the fear of God, and is now expressed in words like faith, love,
thankfulness, and knowledge of God, which are filled with
spiritual tension. For this new way of describing the individual's
right attitude to his God not only expresses that bowing before
the overwhelming majesty of the holy God, which was proclaimed by the prophets with unheard-of passion; but the
strongest possible emphasis falls upon the spiritual initiative of
the individual, which is no purely passive abandonment
but demands a conscious grasp of the newly offered reality
of life.

In the spiritual crisis undergone by the whole national consciousness as a result of this new independence of the individual,
the old national unity was bound to suffer. Its substance had

[18] I Sam. 15.22; Amos 5.21-24; Hos. 6.6; Isa. 1.1-11; Jer. 7.21-23.

in any case been threatened by the penetration of world culture and by a growing social cleavage. But no prophet had ever consented to save the solid national structure by means of a compromise with those powers, whose closed organization offered protection to the national unity and greatness at the expense of the individual's spiritual independence and consciousness of his worth, misusing what was holy for their human ends. The prophets were convinced that they served their people best by risking its outward existence in order to keep it from betrayal of its spiritual birthright for the mess of pottage of political success. And they were ready to pay with their lives for this conviction.

In this struggle, in which the ultimate questions of its spiritual self-understanding were put with extraordinary clarity, Israel's outward fate was sealed. But in what survived of Israel, those goods for which the prophets had fought were maintained with steadfast loyalty, even though the inevitable consequence of Israel's withdrawal from the great stream of world history into the backwater of unpolitical existence as a cult-community was a narrowing of its horizon and a curtailment of its spiritual standards. How important even is the one fact that the priesthood was able to use the varied wealth of the cult to express the great *leitmotiv* that in the realm of Israel everything—space and time, possessions and life—belongs to God alone and is 'hallowed' to him, so that the unity even of the externals of worship is found in the demanding will of the God of the Covenant. There can no longer be any reliance on a mechanical and magical effect in the ritual, for now it shows itself to be the form of life for the people of the covenant which is well-pleasing to God and which summons each individual to deliberate co-operation in humble service. If we add, on the one hand the deepening of the already mentioned conception of the Law,[19] which saw social justice as springing

[19] Cf. p. 12f.

from the most personal expression of love,[20] and on the other hand the energy with which the priestly historians characterized piety as a matter of moral testing by the supreme Judge,[21] then the practical effect of the prophets' struggle in this important realm becomes evident. It is therefore no mere chance that it is the priestly recorder who emphasizes the thought of the divine image in the creation of man, thus providing a definition which can never be lost for all who wear the human face.[22]

What the community of the Law could achieve in its struggle for the individual's understanding of himself appears in the poetry of Job, which was nurtured in its womb. Here is the unique expression of a passionate resistance to the enslaving of man and the stultifying of his relation with God through a petty legalistic theory of retribution.[23]

It may be noted in passing that even the Wisdom literature of Israel, contrary to its original nature, was affected by the same basic tendency. Its cosmopolitan and religiously neutral worldly wisdom, operating mainly on grounds of expediency, changes into a means of obedience to the unquestionable divine command, teaching that true wisdom lies in the fear of God.[24]

In these historical forms, which are so different from one another, we see, therefore, that the fundamental datum of Israel's view of life is that the individual is summoned to a responsibility which demands to be taken as absolute. The man to whom God's demand comes is recognized as a person, an I, who cannot be represented or replaced by any other. Even his belonging to the nation cannot provide him with a cover behind

[20] Lev. 19.18.

[21] They were able to tell, even before the introduction of the cultic code, of a moral change in the patriarchs, and they exclude every characteristic in the national saga which conflicts with their moral ideal.

[22] See below, p. 30f.

[23] Pp. 58f.

[24] Cf. the detailed exposition of J. Fichtner in *Die altorientalische Weisheit in ihrer israelitisch-jüdischen Ausprägung*, 1933, pp. 46ff., 97ff. (Beihefte zur Z.A.W. 62.)

which he might retreat from the divine demand. He is summoned before God as the man he is, and placed before a decision. Here a view of personality is more and more clearly established which has nothing to do with an animistic theory of an indestructible soul-substance, giving man a share in the divine life in virtue of his nature, and thus ensuring meaning to his existence. Nor is it possible here, as in Greek thought, to establish the structure of the human I as a regulated spiritual unity, by analysing and co-ordinating the individual's spiritual forces, which are intended to be harmoniously bound together. But the human person, as a responsibly acting I, responding to the call of the divine Thou by action, possesses its unrepeatable unity and independence only in God's act of election, which summons it to a spiritual communion with him.

4. *The historical character of the relation with God as the basis of a new understanding of history and of time*

From all this wrestling for a proper understanding of the divine claim, in the most different periods and in face of the constantly changing demands of the historical situation, it is clear that there is no rigid, timeless normalization of life, acting like a kind of compulsory religious culture to keep life at a certain level, closed to all historical progress. But because the divine will is understood not as an impersonal law but as a personal will, relation with it does not rule out man's personal existence. But it includes it, and impels man to shape all his relations in responsibility and constant attentiveness to changing historical circumstances. The message which is basic to all action, that God declares a people to be his possession which he draws into communion with him, in order to shape its life anew and distinct from the nations living far from him, presents us with a norm which is not rigid, but elastic. It is a norm which affirms the historical growth even of the chosen people, with all its needs, thus presenting its riches in ever new forms and relations to the changing situation. In brief, God did not simply speak once and proclaim his will, but he speaks again and again to his people and teaches it to see him at work in the course of history, and thus to attack its historical tasks with complete seriousness.

In virtue of this understanding of God's will no flight from history is possible. The Greeks could escape from historical necessity by seeking an abstract, timeless norm which could free them from the concrete connexion of life to the everyday, the individual and the transitory. This norm appeared to them as an unchanging ideal, as a universal image of the perfect man, which in the vicissitudes of history and the pressures of their actual situation could be called their sure and inalienable possession. For this ideal, in accordance with which they shaped their lives into a work of art, is nothing other than the individual application to the human microcosm of the grand universal law which rules the cosmos. In this way the human microcosm is fitted into the unity of the cosmos, and an existence for the individual is made possible, beyond temporal laws, in the sphere of the timeless and eternal.

With the Israelites the situation is quite different. Even though they can see that the goal of history, in the main course of God's action, is the establishment of his lordship, this does not provide them with an insight into the grand universal laws with which the laws of their own life might be harmonized, and thus a proper place in the cosmos asserted for their life.[25] They do not win mastery over the moment, and with it an impregnable position above the rise and fall of history, by foreknowledge of God's will, or a right application of the unchanging eternal norm to the concrete case. Rather, it is into the midst of history with all its insecurity and unforeknowable

[25] Cf. below, p. 28f.

possibilities that God's will leads. It is at a definite point in temporal events, in the here and now, that this will assumes definite and unrecurring form, in which it demands obedience. In such a situation right decision can be reached only if there is constant readiness to listen to the demand which is being made in the situation. Thus at the very beginning the will of the God of Sinai gives directions for the concrete historical situation to the tribes of Israel who had fled from Egypt. This will binds them together in the duty of regulating their common life and of establishing the goal of their wanderings in obedience to the Torah or instructions which are given from time to time through Moses the appointed mediator. And so throughout the future. This Torah, proclaimed now through seers, now through priests or prophets, comes into constant conflict with the natural tendencies first of tribal egoism, then of state power as consolidated in the monarchy, then of the religious impulses which poured themselves out in the service of the cult. The Torah demands readiness for obedient decision. It is characteristic of the Law, which proclaims God's lordship over the whole realm of life, that it does not produce a rounded and well-thought-out system. Any attempt to establish a system of casuistry comprehending every contingency is foreign to it. This has often been regarded as a sign of an unfortunate lack of logical and organizing power. But if we set this lack alongside the desire to derive every individual command from the one great basic command (which we find in Deuteronomy as well as in the levitical law), then we perceive the awareness of God's will as not permitting any fixed anticipation but demanding that it be grasped in ever fresh decision. It asks of the judge a constant openness to the directions which are given to him by the exigencies of the moment. The whole fury of the prophets' criticism of those who are commissioned to foster the divine Law is kindled at the point where these men, judges or priests or prophets, 'handle the law without knowing Yahweh' (Jer. 2.8). These believe that everything is done if they have the superficial knowledge and make a routine application of the formal Law. Proud of their perfect professional technique, they show no inner readiness to learn anew the 'Thou shalt' which is demanded of them in the moment. Thus they also lead astray those who rely on them, to trust in 'the precept of men' (Isa. 29.13), in which 'the heart is far from God'. That is, the ever new divine summons is ignored. Yet it is only in this conscious responsibility to the concrete moment, with its unforeseeable demand, that man is able to affirm that personal value which God desires to give to him, thus realizing the destiny which gives his life both a content and a goal. In this way man is able to understand God's continuous action towards him, in which God shows himself as a real 'Other', and in the inexhaustible possibilities of his living power and in his never weary loyalty guides man to the accomplishment of his aims for the world.

It is evident that there is no room in this view for a self-contained and harmoniously rounded life, for the shaping of personality into a work of art in accordance with the demands of the ideal of the *kalon kagathon*. It has been rightly observed that the Old Testament has no heroes or saints. It is too vividly aware of God's constant questioning of man, and calling him in question, to allow any confidence to be established in an ideal image of human personality at rest in itself. History is a movement effected by God which challenges man and gives him his destiny and his task. In this situation time cannot become a matter of indifference, as merely the material form of life over which rises, as man's real home, the reality of the spirit with its regular and ordered world. But time becomes rather the unrecurring reality which is given by God and which urges man to a decision; the reality which inexorably calls for a decision here and now and permits no rests in some secure position which is valid once for all.

THE COSMIC EXTENT AND RICH CONTENT OF MAN'S RELATION WITH GOD ON THE BASIS OF BELIEF IN THE CREATOR

1. *Belief in the Creator as a revelation of man's dependence and dignity*

(*a*) The view of human life which we have so far depicted is certainly not present with equal clarity in all parts of the Old Testament. Its effects, however, are present in all parts. It attained both width and fullness through close association with the belief in the Creator. The Lawgiver, under whose authority all life is placed, is recognized and worshipped not only as the Lord of the nation who had been revealed in history, but also as the Creator of the world, and 'there is none beside him'. His will with its ordering and demanding power therefore appears in a new light. First, it is less possible than ever for anybody to escape his responsibility towards God. For now the order of the national life is determined by the same will as reigns throughout the universe and imposes its laws upon it. There is no escape in any direction from this iron ring.

It is characteristic of Israel's thought of the Creator that it does not tempt us to construct a new relation between man and God by supposing a physical or spiritual kinship between Creator and creature. It does not make the bold attempt to fathom the being of the Creator from a knowledge of the visible creation, and to penetrate into his workshop. The ground is taken away from under such an attempt by the very fact that the Creator of whom the Old Testament witnesses speak is not the constructor of the world, the demiurge who forms the world from primal matter which is already there, as depicted in creation-myths of the ancient east.[1] Nor is he the world-principle which seems to the reason to be indispensable for explaining the world. But he is, rather, over against the world as the Transcendent One whose ground of life is in himself, completely independent of the world's existence, and who calls the cosmos into existence as the free establishment of his will. This divine will keeps its secret; in its secret hiddenness it remains impenetrable and does not yield itself to his creatures as the ground of being which is accessible to the human spirit. But it never ceases to hold before the human spirit its separation from the 'wholly other'. This excludes the possibility of deriving the law of one's being from universal law, or of understanding it as a special case within the general order. Nor can man, as a creature, have the world at his disposal in thought, but he is completely at the mercy of the divine Lord of the world. Every attempt to spy out this Lord's plans, and to derive the reasonableness of the world's laws and the perfection of the Lawgiver from the harmony of the whole world as grasped by the human mind, is bound to come to grief on the absolute lordship of the Creator. From the primeval creation story of the Yahwist in Gen. 2 to the Psalms of the creation, such as Ps. 8, 19, 29, 104 and 148, and the priestly account of the creation in Gen. 1, this understanding of the creature remains unaltered, until its classic expression in the speeches of the Lord in the Book of Job.[2]

(*b*) That the creature is given no chance of escaping from its creaturely dependence, and of making man's position secure in face of the Creator's power to have him at his disposal, is, however, only one side of the Old Testament understanding of the

---

[1] Cf. the Song of the Creation, 'As above', and other creation stories, in *Altorientalische Texte zum Alten Testament*, ed. H. Gressmann, 2nd ed. 1926, pp. 119ff.

[2] Cf. my *Theologie des Alten Testaments*, II, 49ff. and 77ff.

creature. The other side, which is inextricably bound up with the first, becomes plain in the fact that all the Old Testament witnesses we have mentioned also speak of a unique connexion of the incomprehensible and mysterious Creator with his creature—though of a connexion established not by man but by God alone. It consists of God's honouring man, and him alone of all creatures, by addressing him and confronting him as a 'Thou'. As One who offers himself for communion he emerges from his hiddenness into a morally positive relation with his creature, in which he shows him his special place and task in the world. As a creature man is ranged with all other creatures, but now, as the one whom God's Word meets, he comes to God's side and confronts the rest of creation. Man is not simply a piece of nature, however firmly interwoven his life is in the order of nature. In the time of ancient Israel the relation of man and the world is grounded in the thought of his lordship over the creatures. But because this destiny of the weak and totally dependent creature is understood as a miracle of the unquestionable divine will of the Creator, Israel is not led astray into *hubris*, but moved to adoring praise of the wisdom of the Creator, as expressed, for instance, in Ps. 8. The earlier account of the creation (Gen. 2) ascribes the clear boundary between man and the animals, which prevents man from finding his complement and completion in the sub-human creation, to the effects of man's independent spiritual nature, by which he is set on God's side. In man's destiny as being made in the image of God, the priestly thinker, however, brings together the sayings about man's special place in the creation[3] and gives pregnant utterance to the thought that man cannot be submerged in nature or merged in the laws of the cosmos, so long as he remains true to his destiny. The Creator's greatest gift to man, that of the personal I, necessarily places him, in analogy with God's being, at a distance from nature.

[3] Gen. 1.26f.

Is it surprising that this view of man's place in the world gives rise to a rapture which finds powerful expression in hymns of praise,[4] and even in the apparently sober and formal priestly account of the creation leaves some traces of the thrill of joyous adoration and admiration? The mysterious grandeur of nature and the autonomy of its laws are preserved. But its hostility and strangeness are abolished—those alien qualities which terrified primitive man, who saw nature as the abode of uncanny spirits and powers, amid which he was only with difficulty able to assert himself. When nature lost its gods that myth-making fantasy came to an end, which had bound man to the dark instinctive life of the plant and animal world and by uniting him mystically to the power of nature had prevented the development of his personal spiritual being. In face of this liberation the burden of responsibility and his limited and conditioned life as a creature cease to oppress him. For this liberation brings with it a share in the divine life and work, in which man appears as the goal of creation and is set in the centre of the universe.

This is not to say that man now simply has nature at his disposal. The world of creation has its own laws, which regulate the marvellous play of forces among the elemental powers, as well as the life and activity of the animal world, and are far beyond man's understanding.[5] It is true that even the incomprehensible terrors in the life of nature cannot call man's divine destiny in question when these terrors are understood as an indication of the glory of the Creator. It is only when a lively sense of the living rule of the godhead in the mighty course of natural forces is obscured by later rational reflection, which attempts, in its own strength, to illuminate the relation between the life of man and of nature, that the autonomy of nature's

---

[4] Cf. Ps. 19; 29; 104; 135; 147.

[5] Job 38ff. Cf. also the ordering of the life of nature by divine command in the account of creation in Gen. 1, and the praise of the cosmic wisdom, which is inaccessible to man, in Job 28.12ff. and Prov. 8.22ff.

laws is raised to alien and uncanny power. The regularity of natural phenomena becomes a monotonous mechanism, whose course yields no answer to the question of the meaning of man's life, but is in the last resort aimless and leaves questioning man weary and disillusioned.[6]

This great increase in the distance between man and nature but serves to make clear the decisive significance of the Old Testament consciousness of election for the Israelite view of nature. For everywhere else the strangeness of the life of nature, even when it is clearly experienced, is modified in a peculiar manner by the certainty that behind nature stands the same Lord who has revealed himself in history as the One who has chosen his people. And we find expressed not only adoring wonder at the mysterious power of the Creator, wonder which conquers all slavish fear of the riddles of the universe beyond man; but also the consciousness of a responsibility which shows man his attitude to the uncomprehended special areas of creation. He is not given unlimited use either of the animal world or of the land. Rather, it is one of his duties to respect their special life and to submit to the order of creation which shows him his limits.[7] The life of nature is most firmly related to responsible human action when Canaan is dignified with the title of the divine inheritance, enjoining on man a certain behaviour lest he defile the land and be spat out by it.[8]

Thus, then, the will of the God of Israel as Redeemer is one with his will as Creator. That is why the psalms can speak in

[6] This is very clearly emphasized in the sayings of Ecclesiastes.

[7] Ex. 23.19; Lev. 19.19; Deut. 22.9ff.; Job 31.38, 40. On the latter point cf. Duhm's exposition (*Das Buch Hiob*, 1897, in K.H.C. ed. Marti, Sect. XVI), which I think rightly deletes verse 39 as a late gloss. Of course we are not concerned here with the origin of such commandments in the history of religion, but with their significance in the Old Testament understanding of God's will.

[8] So especially in Deuteronomy, which gives, however, precise expression to moods which were current in Israel long before Deuteronomy. Cf. Jer. 2.7; 3.1f.; 9; 16.18; Lev. 18.25, 27f.; 20.22.

the same breath in praise and adoration—apparently quite spontaneously and yet with profound significance—of God's mighty deeds in nature and of his redemptive deeds in Israel.[9] That is why the Psalmist of the 104th Psalm can describe nature as the divine home in which man feels at ease, and can employ his energies adequately. This employment, in fact, corresponds so admirably to man's nature that in Paradise it was his natural activity. As guardian and cultivator of the garden of Eden Adam is destined to work, though without the curse of great toil which came later as a result of his disobedience.[10] So the conclusion of the later creation-story sketches in a few words a programme of human history and culture, when it describes man's divine commission as to replenish the earth and to have dominion over the creatures.[11] It is no accident that this commission is summarized in a blessing. God's will presents man's goal to him, and desires that he prosper and spread. Only godlessness prevents men from prospering : 'The godless know not salvation.'[12]

When man's cultural task is so energetically affirmed, it is only logical that the natural and cultural goods which are indispensable to the community should have an important place among the goals of moral action. Indeed, it is this exaltation, in the Old Testament, of earthly possessions, many children, long life, friendship and love, as well as wisdom, beauty, honour and political freedom, which is a continual thorn in the flesh for a spiritual view of life, and causes it to regard Old Testament morality as inferior. But it is also evident that where the unconditioned demand of the Creator's will is laid upon the existence of an actual people in its concrete reality, it is not possible for that will to be indifferent to the natural foundations of life. This is all the less possible when the man on whom God's demand is laid is man seen in his spiritual and physical

[9] Ps. 24; 135; 136; 147; 148.
[10] Gen. 2.15.
[11] Gen. 1.28.
[12] Isa. 48.22; 57.21.

c

wholeness. In this situation it is not possible, as it is in various versions of idealism, for the natural physical life to be contrasted with the spiritual life, the latter alone being granted value, and an assured and invulnerable existence, while the former is regarded as inferior and unimportant for the realization of life's goal. Nor is Israel's view a vestigial primitive conception which has not been completely overcome—which is the apology frequently made on behalf of Israel. But Israel's realism is closely bound up both with God's will as Lord, experienced as an obligation, and with his will as Creator, which is included in this. It is therefore a realism which is bound to make its influence irresistibly felt where man's unconditional responsibility is seen as grounded in this divine will.[13]

When human life is thus surrounded and upheld by God's blessed will, man's basic mood in relation to his task and his destiny is one of joy. As God's pleasure in his works is recounted in psalms[14] which but repeat the praise and jubilation of the morning stars and all the sons of God on the morning of creation,[15] which in fact see the world as a joyous game of God's wisdom,[16] so joy is seen as man's portion from God.[17] In particular, joy is a mark of the divine service and the festivals in the Temple, where God's mercy is praised.[18] And God is besought to confirm this gift in days of tribulation, as a sign of his new-given mercy.[19] The ideal reign of Solomon finds no better description than as a time of universal and unimpaired joyousness.[20] The irruption of the age of salvation is also bound

[13] On this question of the goods of life, see further pp. 46ff.

[14] Ps. 104.31; cf. Gen. 1, with its emphasis on 'And God saw that it was good'.

[15] Job 38.7.

[16] Prov. 8.22-31.

[17] Eccl. 2.26; 8.15; 9.7; 11.9f.

[18] Deut. 12.7, 12, 18; 14.26; 16.11, 14; 26.11; 27.7; Lev. 23.40; Num. 10.10.

[19] Ps. 5.12; 14.7; 35.9; 40.17; 51.105.

[20] I Kings 4.20.

up with the awakening of great joy.[21] 'No other word is so central to the Old Testament as joy.'[22] Joy is the fine expression of what it meant for the Old Testament understanding of man that Israel's consciousness of election, by its connexion with the belief in the Creator, was opened to the width and richness of the world of creation.

2. *Belief in the Creator as the basis of social thought*

If man's destiny in creation draws an ineffaceable line between man and the world, on the other hand it draws men together among themselves, and takes away the dangerous power of division and destructive hostility which is inherent in the difference between the sexes and between races. The division of mankind into man and woman is certainly not treated lightly in the Old Testament, but its effects are clearly to be seen in the patriarchal system with its relegation of women to the background. All the more noteworthy is the equality, in principle, of men and women before God, whether, as in the older tradition, the woman appears as man's complement and completion, destined by God,[23] or whether she too is recognized as made in the image of God and thus as sharing in man's special position *vis-à-vis* nature.[24] This admittedly provides no practical solution to the question of our personal destiny. The Israelite writer has nevertheless succeeded in presenting the relationship between the sexes as a profound problem.[25] And at least certain perilous by-ways in the solving of this problem are closed from the very start, and marriage is given a place amongst the divinely ordained social relationships for which man knows he has to account to God.

[21] Isa. 9.2; 86.4; 90.13-15, etc.
[22] L. Koehler, *Theologie des Alten Testaments*, 1936, p. 137.
[23] Gen. 2.18.   [24] Gen. 1.27.   [25] Gen. 2 and 3.

This Old Testament thought of man's creatureliness leads also to the clear grasp of the concept of humanity, which is quite distinct from the view generally held among ancient peoples. As creatures of the one God the peoples are members of one great family, and the list of the nations in Gen. 10, which is unique in ancient Eastern literature, includes Israel, proudly conscious though it is of its preferential historical position, in the general context of humanity. No claim is made for Israel of any fundamentally different natural capacity or 'inherited nobility' which might set it apart from the rest of the nations. The Old Testament knows nothing of races which are 'naturally inferior' or unworthy of designation as human, just as the dividing wall between Greeks and barbarians, or between master races and slave natures, which was never wholly overcome in the ancient world, is completely foreign to it. Even the most exclusive Old Testament writer, the priestly recorder, recognizes that the heathen peoples are also set in a direct relation with God and have a similar responsibility to him, which the writer expresses in the same word, 'covenant', which is decisive for Israel's relation with God.[26] And as mankind appears at the beginning of Israel's records as a single entity, so too, in Israel's view of the future, mankind appears as the united community of nations receiving God's new world, and thus returning to their origin.[27]

The unique strength of this universal view of mankind appears in its avoiding of two pressing dangers. First, it does not get lost in a perverted cosmopolitanism, to which the individual's responsibility to his own nation is a matter of indifference. And second, it is not destroyed by an exaggerated nationalism, which often blazes up in Israel as a consequence of political misfortunes. The decisive factor in the overcoming of the first danger was the remarkable combination of individual

[26] Gen. 9.1-17.
[27] Isa. 2.2-4; Zech. 9.9f.; Zeph. 3.9; Isa. 45.22-24, etc.

responsibility and national life, to which we have already referred.[28] For on the one hand this combination summoned the individual to willing participation in the natural forms of society, marriage, family, people and State, where he could realize the divine order and take his share in shaping the holy people desired by God. Not love of the world in general, but love of his neighbour, is what the Israelite had to confirm in his actual situation in the midst of the people; and for this love of the near no love of those far away can be a substitute. In this situation cosmopolitanism would be disloyalty and disobedience.[29]

Nor on the other hand is it possible for the individual to become shut up in himself, and to achieve a private and isolated relation between God and the soul. Even the powerful summons to the individual which is found in the prophetic proclamation, and which sets the individual, in certain circumstances, quite alone, in opposition to the whole people, never for one moment questioned the fact that God's action is directed towards a community and seeks the individual as a member of this community. The intensive relation of the individual life to God, therefore, does not lead to ascetic forms of life which separate the *homo religiosus*, the religious virtuoso, from the crowd, and make concentration on his high goal easier for him. However true it is that the prophetic movement—with its exponents clad in raw hide, and separated from their earlier callings in order to sit at the feet of some famous master— recalls ascetic motives, yet it demands of its members neither poverty nor celibacy, and it does not join with the sect of the Rechabites in their scorn of agriculture.[30] That romantic dream of a renewal of the ancient forms of life, which might make easier the decision for God, never gained favour with the

[28] Cf. p. 16ff.
[29] Lev. 19.18 and 34 are the most unambiguous formulation of this. Cf. Ex. 23.4f.; Deut. 22.1-4.
[30] Cf. Jer. 35.1ff.

prophets. Rather they lead one to grasp the Creator's will even in the richer context of life, in its actual demand on each individual, and so to penetrate to a radical renewal of the whole of life.

The danger to this universal view of mankind is greater from the side of national exclusiveness and arrogance. It is true that election by the God of the Covenant never leaves any doubt that the national life must also be completely subservient to the religious task, and is unable to make any independent demands in face of the claims of the divine Lord for absolute obedience. But the national successes in the period of the monarchy, with the consequent strengthening of national feelings, tempted the people again and again to understand the promise of the Covenant as a guarantee of national claims and to misuse it for the religious glorification of royal power politics. The part played in the royal psalms by the military defeat and humiliation of the nations is characteristic of this misuse of the Covenant.[31] The danger was that the exalted divine Lord might be reduced to the petty and limited status of a national god who is by nature able to bring nothing but salvation to his people and nothing but destruction to his people's foes. That is the reason for the bitter struggle waged by the prophets against a monarchy which claimed that its narrow-minded national policy was God's will, and identified the goal of the divine government of the world with the glorification of Israel. The terrible confirmation of the prophets' side in this political struggle, through the collapse of the State and the exile of the people, gave full rein to the universal way of thinking, and led the historians to their thoroughgoing criticism of every misuse of the thought of election for national deification. Stories like those of Ruth and Jonah show with what strength the heathen too are drawn into God's sway. The Book of Job, which discusses the deepest problems of Edomite and Arabian sages, also shows the effect of belief in the universal Creator. The psalms which glorify

[31] Cf. Ps. 2.9ff.; 21.9ff.; 45.6; 110.5ff.

the world-embracing kingship of the God of Israel, also allow room in the worship of God for the thought of the universal kingdom of God.[32] It is true that nationalist and particularist streams mingle with the hopes of the post-exilic community.[33] But prophecies like those contained in Joel, Malachi and the Little Apocalypse (Isa. 24-27), bear witness to the continuance of that hope of salvation for all the world, in the last period of Israel's history, and keep the Old Testament understanding of man untainted by the lofty arrogance of the hereditary nobility.

[32] Ps. 93; 96; 97; 99.
[33] Isa. 65f.; Zech. 9.11-11.3; 12.1ff.; Obad. 15ff.

CHAPTER THREE

THE ANTINOMIES OF THE
UNCONDITIONAL OUGHT

In view of the attitude of Israel to the goods of life one could be tempted to define the Old Testament understanding of life in terms of a naïve and completely earthbound optimism, innocent of any depths of reflection. But this would take into account only one aspect of this remarkable understanding of the self. To grasp Israel's position properly, we must also take another aspect into account.

For it is not only the 'ought' which stands over human life with an all-embracing and unconditional obligation, and gives life direction, as we have tried to show. But the things which contradict this 'ought'—which arise from the natural conditions of human existence and from the spiritual character of the individual—are also seen with the same realism, and confronted with the goal which is set to human life.

1. Hindrances arising from the natural life of the nation

The connexion of the individual with his people was particularly strong in Israel, as we have seen,[1] since it was in the natural

---

[1] See p. 16f. and 33.

community that the unconditioned divine Ought showed him his duties and made him aware of a great divinely-willed task. It was in fact for the sake of this task that the individual possessed the right of free access to the God who had chosen Israel. This must have struck him all the more since early in Israel's history it became apparent that, from purely natural considerations, Israel possessed only limited suitability for the attainment of the absolute goal.

Thought in terms of the nation was certainly limited from the start by the fact that it was not the nation as such which was declared to be the goal of the will, nor the service of the nation's power and greatness the supreme law. Even the nation which grew out of the union of the tribes was placed from the beginning beneath a higher purpose, a ruling idea, that of the realization of a religious task. The outward sign of this was the sacred Covenant of the tribes, which traced its origin to the experience at Sinai. This Israelite amphictyony gathered round a sanctuary and upheld, as the order for Israel's life, the Law of the God of the Covenant who was worshipped by the whole people. It was the realization of this order which formed the foundation of the common life. 'Let my people go, that they may serve me', is the recurrent formula of an old historian for God's demand of Pharaoh,[2] and this gives classic expression to the purpose of Israel's election. The consciousness of this primarily religious task was not extinguished in the course of the centuries, as we may see from the remarkable fact that long after the covenantal form of life had been replaced by the monarchial State, the Laws were handed down as ordinances of this Covenant and not as royal laws.[3] It was as proclamations of the will of the divine Lord of the Covenant that they were accepted as binding.

[2] Ex. 7.16; 9.13; 10.3.
[3] Martin Noth has rightly drawn attention to this point, though his conclusions from it are not always tenable (*Die Gesetze im Pentateuch*, 1940, p. 9ff.).

This has often been regarded as nothing more than the religious glorification of the people's natural will to live. But this view does not pay sufficient attention to the fact that the religious aim of the national life often conflicted, at decisive points, with the national egoism, and could be effected only by a hard struggle. Neither the words, 'My country right or wrong', nor 'The good is what benefits the people', can become the dominant maxim. Rather, the individual's unconditioned responsibility must appear in his being able to represent that Law of God which is over the people, even by his opposition to the people, and see in this his call to personal service of the whole community.

In the early period it is true that this conflict only rarely broke out. At that time the people's faith was the strongest motivating force of national unity, and it was in the summons to the war of Yahweh that the national unity, which surpassed all centrifugal tribal interests, became most evident—as we may see, for instance, in the old song in Judg. 5.[4] Nevertheless, in individual decisions, as in the question of confederation or expulsion, the opposition of the divine Law to the natural self-assertiveness of the nation could become evident—as is reflected in the very oldest sagas.[5] But it was with the national unification under the monarchy that the possibilities of conflict became greatest. For now a separate political will could rebel against the religious goal, while at the same time the differentiation in culture encouraged an attack upon the old norms of the Law as being burdensome shackles on progress.[6] Here true service of the people involved a bitter struggle with the natural representatives of the national will—the king and his officials, the priests

---

[4] Cf. especially 5.2, 4, 9, 11, 23, 31, but also Judg. 6.18, and the title of the old book of songs quoted in Num. 21.14—'the book of the wars of the Lord.'

[5] Cf. Ex. 32; Num. 14.39ff.; 16; Josh. 9; Judg. 19-21.

[6] Cf. B. Balscheit and W. Eichrodt, *Die soziale Botschaft des Alten Testaments für die Gegenwart*, p. 42ff.

and prophets of the State religion. As a result of the prophets' efforts this struggle led to the utter surrender of the national life, which had been untrue to its real destiny. From Elijah onwards—with whom we see the first indications of this terrible result[7]—the end of the nation appears ever more clearly to the great messengers of God as the inevitable result of failure to serve him, as we may see in the writings of Amos and his successors.

For the individual member of the nation this end to the struggle was a threat to the very roots of his existence; and the painful divisions and distractions which seized him are clearly reflected in the lament of Baruch and in the promise of his friend Jeremiah.[8] In the Book of Ezekiel,[9] too, in the words of the prophet himself as well as in the bearing of the exiled Jews, there are clear echoes of these experiences. The work of the prophets, it is true, prepared a shelter for the individual which helped him to bear the heavy burden laid upon him by the prophets' judgements—the shelter of a close association, namely, with those who were ready for repentance and new obedience. In Isaiah's prophetic influence the decisive point is reached when with a grave warning he turns away from the unrepentant people, who are on the brink of disaster, and a circle of disciples appears. This circle is formed round God's messenger, having decided with him against the nation's ruinous self-will.[10] Since the life-bringing Word of God is entrusted to the prophet, and withheld from his obstinate opponents, it is to him that God's decree of salvation, effective even in judgement, is directed. Here is Israel *kata pneuma*, the people of God living not by common blood but by faith in the Word, the people which God will use as the cornerstone for the new building of his kingdom.[11] This separation from the national community is

---

[7] Cf. I Kings 19.14ff.   [10] Isa. 8.1, 2, 16.
[8] Jer. 45.   [11] Isa. 28.16.
[9] Ezek. 9.8; 11.13; 18.2, 5, 29; 21.12; 24.15ff.; 33.10.

not effected by an arbitrary smashing of national barriers, but by obedience to the rule and judgement of God, who takes his revelation away from an unreceptive people and entrusts it to the congregation (*Gemeinde*).[12] For it is the Church which may be seen in embryo here, and in waiting for the fulfilment of God's Word it has its proper function.[13] It is in the congregation that Jeremiah shows his exiled fellow-countrymen in Babylon the possibility of living a life of obedience to God's commands and of participation in his blessing even without the protective framework of State and nation.[14] With untiring energy Ezekiel labours to weld the aimless flock of exiles into a congregation of God possessing in the Law the infallible guide for their life and an effective protection from the heathen world around them.[15] In the Jewish community (*Gemeinde*) which was established in Jerusalem by Ezra and Nehemiah under the aegis of the Persian State, the new form of life for God's people seemed at last to be realized: by surrendering the national framework, with all its inadequacies and temptations, this community could put its untrammelled energies into the religious task which had formerly been assigned to the whole nation.

And yet this new form of life never succeeded in being established as the full solution of the problem as to the true people of God. The Jewish community was dominated by the hope of again becoming a people who might fulfil their destiny better than the first people had done, even though they no longer aimed at realizing this hope by their own efforts. Even those

---

[12] The word *Gemeinde* has been translated variously in this passage as 'congregation', 'Church' and 'community'. 'Congregation' is the most natural rendering, yet perhaps in the context the most likely to mislead English readers. The author is thinking of the religious community (or the Church) as distinct from the whole people—Translators' Note.

[13] Isa. 8.17f., 19f.; cf. 7.9.

[14] Jer. 29.

[15] Cf. especially Ezek. 3.16ff.; 14; 18; 20.

prophets whose influence had contributed most to the consolidation of the new common life in Jerusalem, Haggai and Zechariah, saw the goal of God's rule to be a new people under his Saviour-king.[16]   Thus they regarded the restored worshipping community, with its high priest, as an interim structure in whose place the real divine building would some day be raised.   Only in that people of the future, which as a new creation of God would bear wonderful marks upon it, did it seem possible for the destiny of individual life also to be realized.

Thus, on the basis of the knowledge of God which had been vouchsafed to it, the thought of Israel clung tenaciously and with tough realism to the image of the full man which was guaranteed to it by its own eternal destiny as a people.   It preferred an unsatisfied 'Not yet' to giving up its belief in the fulfilment of the original will of God.   The Israelite understanding of existence had therefore to pass through the most severe and shattering questioning in order to make plain that the establishment of the unconditional Ought means the destruction of the natural conditions of life, and the leading of man into a merely provisional form of existence, whose meaning consists in its pointing something still to come, and still veiled, towards which the will turns in tense expectation.

2. *Hindrances arising from the attitude to natural goods*

A similar process is fulfilled in the evaluation of natural goods. In connexion with the thought of creation we have already had occasion to note the appreciative attitude shown by Israelite thought to every kind of life's goods.[17]   These remarks must

[16] Hag. 2.20ff.; Zech. 3.8; 6.9ff.; 8.7f., 13.
[17] See p. 33f.

now be completed by our noting that the gifts of the Creator were not only appreciated, but they were at the same time called in question by the unconditioned Ought. It is characteristic that this questioning of the goods of life, in the same way as the treasuring of them, is determined by the experience of God's personal action upon man. It is not the hostile moods of a primitive level of life which lead to the sacrifice of cultural goods.[18] The duty of sacrificing possessions and earthly happiness is, rather, passionately apprehended where the call to battle sounds forth among the tribes on behalf of the God of the Covenant and his lordship, whether threatened by foes without or foes within.[19] It is there that to avoid suffering by holding fast to external advantages and securities means disloyalty, and betrayal of the supreme norm of life.[20] It is true that this intermittent testing of unconditional surrender to God's demand does not question the naïve conjunction of external blessing with the attitude to the Covenant: in the normal course of things piety and earthly happiness form a single assured unity.

It is a more profound observation that it is the man with special gifts who is often specially exposed to the temptation of wantonly scorning God's will. Thus it was with Absalom, winning hearts with his youthful beauty;[21] with Achitophel, famed for his intelligence;[22] with Michal, a king's daughter, proud of her royal lineage;[23] with the rich sheep-owner Nabal,[24] and so on. And as the favourite is in greater danger of a great fall, so the neglected one may often have the surprising

[18] It is wrong to seek something of this kind in the Yahwist's account of Paradise in Gen. 2f., which would trivialize the point of the conflict which he depicts. Such motives are more readily to be found among the sect of the Rechabites, who cling to the cultural level of the nomadic cattle-breeders; but the Rechabites never had any strong influence on Israel. See above, p. 37.

[19] Ex. 32.25ff.; Judg. 5; 19-21.
[20] Judg. 5.15ff., 23; I Sam. 11.7.
[21] II Sam. 14.25; 15.1ff.
[22] II Sam. 16.23.
[23] II Sam. 6.16, 20.
[24] I Sam. 25.

experience that God is watching over him and leading him to the heights of life.[25]   Thus at an early period there is a lively understanding that earthly happiness and divine pleasure are not simply identical, however naïvely the one is often seen in the other, but can often be fiercely opposed.   There is therefore a clear limit to the positive appreciation of life's goods.

If the whole life, being thus directed towards the divine Lord of the people, formed a protection against primitive eudaemonism (for which a crude or a refined enjoyment of life is the ultimate goal), likewise the severe crisis which overshadowed the whole nation in the period of the late monarchy urged upon Israel new reflection concerning the meaning of the natural goods of life.   The increasing richness and brilliance of external life had by no means been accompanied by happiness.   But these had heightened and sharpened the contrasts in society and thereby destroyed the ancient national unity.   An easy life of enjoyment was now possible, and satisfaction of an egoistic lust for power and pleasure became the goal of many lives.   At the same time justice and morality went by the board, and unscrupulous plundering of one's neighbours was a common event. The prophets, heedless of consequences to themselves, exposed this betrayal of the divine destiny of the people, and showed that the terrible consequence of the dissolution of the bond of loyalty to God was the destruction of the nation.   They impressed on each individual his responsibility for this fate, and summoned him to decide against the wrong road taken by the great mass of the people.   In this way they compelled him to see the danger to life of those coveted cultural and natural goods, and to recognize for himself, and to wrestle with, the hard choice between them and unclouded fellowship with God. Here the natural harmony between the outer and the inner life, between nature and spirit, was broken, and there followed a general devaluation of the gifts of creation in face of the one

[25] Hannah, I Sam. if., David in flight, I Sam. 22ff., etc.

infinitely valuable and irreplaceable good, the community of the will with God.

This good now appears with new clarity as a reality which claims and motivates the whole inner life. The God who bears up his own with the strong love of a father, and wishes to surround them with the tender love of a mother, with a true husband's love, who follows his wandering children with deep grief, and out of sheer goodness seeks to draw them to himself —in the prophetic witness this God confronts the individual member of the nation, too, with power.[26] He reveals himself to the individual's inmost desires and feelings as the liberating and renewing power of life which wins from man the venture of faith—to leave all earthly security and cling to God's Word alone,[27] which invites him to forget himself in a love of the whole heart and soul.[28] Here are revealed the riches of a spiritual and moral world, which show themselves independent of all earthly goods and can be experienced in living reality as the true supreme value.

That is why the prophets did not hesitate to promise these riches to those who, as a consequence of the perversion of the divine order of life, had fallen victims to crude and violent men. It is the poor and outwardly needy among the people towards whom God's special solicitude is directed.[29] It is they who are exalted as the real core of the divine community, above those who live in thoughtless riches and enjoyment of every kind, and are made the heirs of the promised divine glory.[30] It is therefore with these that the higher spiritual and moral life of com-

[26] Isa. 1.2; Hos. 11.1, 3; Jer. 3.4, 19; 31.9, 20; Deut. 1.31; 8.5; 32.18; Mal. 1.6; Isa. 49.15; Hos. 2.21f.; 3.1ff.; 6.4; 11.8ff.; 14.5; Jer. 2.2; 3.1ff., 12ff., 22ff.; 4.1; 31.3ff.
[27] Isa. 7.9; 28.16; 30.15; Hab. 2.2-4; Jer. 5.1; Zeph. 3.2, 11f.; Isa. 40.31; 49.23; 57.13.
[28] Hos. 2.22; 4.1; 6.6; 13.4; Jer. 9.22f.; 2.2; Deut. 6.5; 10.12ff.; 11.1.
[29] Amos 8.4; Isa. 3.14f.; 10.2; 11.4; 14.32; 29.19; Micah 2.8f.; 3.3; Jer. 22.16; Zeph. 2.3; Ezra 16.49; Zech. 7.10.
[30] Isa. 14.39; 11.4; 29.19f.; 28.12; Micah 3.3; 4.6f.; Zeph. 3.12.

munity with God reaches its full reality, while those who are richly blessed with all life's goods have in reality lost their life.

The powerful effect on future thought of this paradoxical reversal of the natural concepts of happiness and unhappiness is seen at its most impressive in the fact that the words for poor and wretched become names of honour for the pious. In the language of prayer those words, which originally referred to economic and social need, assume the meaning of the right attitude to God, in humility and trust. The poor are now those who are well-pleasing to God, who just because they are poor may be consoled by the divine favour and blessing.[31] The consciousness of a supreme good which no external fate could assail, an inner happiness which no earthly happiness could replace, is vividly expressed in the Psalms[32] and in the Wisdom literature,[33] and most powerfully of all in the Book of Job.[34] The final consequence of this conviction is drawn by the witnesses who maintain this happiness as indestructible even in face of death.[35]

But the remarkable thing is that this general devaluation of earthly goods by no means leads to a withdrawal from earthly life in which natural enjoyment is regarded as something inferior, if not indeed a temptation, which must be overcome by ascetic renunciation. Such recourse to acosmic efforts to find salvation are foreign to the whole of the Old Testament.[36] The surrender of earthly goods for the sake of inner riches remains a solution of expediency for one who is oppressed by the problems of this world. This does not have the significance of a logical rejection of natural life, so that poverty, say, could be simply classified as the form of life pleasing to God. The figure

[31] Ps. 9.13; 10.2, 9; 14.6; 25.16; 35.10; 74.21; 86.1; 88.16; 109.22.
[32] Ps. 4.8; 16.5ff.; 17.14f.; 23; 36.10; 42.5; 51.14; 63.4; 73.23ff.; 84.11.
[33] Prov. 8.35f.; 102.11; 11.4; 13.12, 14; 14.27.
[34] Job 16.19; 19.25ff.; 38-42. Cf. p. 6of.
[35] Ps. 16; 49; 73. Cf. p. 61f.
[36] See above, p. 37.

D

of the hermit, fleeing the world, or the begging monk, to be found in every cultural religion, never appears within the Old Testament framework of existence. The divine affirmation of creation and its goods as the foundation of the Old Testament understanding of life has clearly penetrated too deeply for decision against them to appear anything but contradictory and paradoxical; and no simply valid form of life can be built up on the basis of such a decision. Thus the prophets regarded their very struggle against the perils and temptations of the goods of creation as a necessary stage towards a new harmony in which an enjoyment of extreme luxury in every area of the natural life would attest anew the richness and goodness of the Creator.[37] And when, in the words salvation, peace,[38] or help, deliverance,[39] they comprehend the whole wealth of the divine blessing, the blessings of earthly life are joined in one great unity with the supreme good of fellowship with God.

The original unity of life, in contrast with the present actuality, is still more strongly maintained where the life of a people living in unclouded covenantal grace is unfolded, as in the Deuteronomic and priestly codes; or where it is desired as in the Wisdom literature to give instruction in the practical mastery of life's problems, on the basis of the divine Wisdom provided in the Law. But here too we are always aware of the smashing of all life's earthly foundations by God's judgement, even though this happens only in extreme cases. This is the warning sign on the horizon of the community which lives by the Law, as is shown by the terrible imprecatory chapters of the Laws.[40] In the circles of the Wisdom teachers, however, in sharp opposition to the self-satisfied cleverness which imagines it can master

[37] Amos 9.12f.; Hos. 2.23f.; Isa. 11.6ff.; 32.15ff.; Jer. 30.18ff.; 31.12ff.; Ezek. 34.25ff., etc.
[38] Hebrew *shalom*, cf. Isa. 9.5f.; Jer. 29.11; 33.9; Isa. 48.18; 53.8.
[39] Hebrew *yesha, yeshuah, t·shuah*, cf. Isa. 45.8, 17; 46.13; 49.6, 8; 51.6, 8.
[40] Deut. 28.15ff.; Lev. 26.14ff.

every riddle of the universe with the aid of a primitive theory of retribution and theodicy,[41] there arose the writer of Job and the destructive criticism of Ecclesiastes. The experience of the incomprehensible majesty of the God of the universe, who does not degrade himself to be the servant of the petty interests of puffed-up mannikins, impels them to deal mortal blows at the alleged harmony in the present state of the world. They teach that the unity of Creator and Redeemer is a truth not open to the reason, which only faith can maintain, grasped and borne up by the eternal divine will.[42] But even where the eudaemonistic union of piety and earthly happiness lives on in the Jewish community, its unnatural defensive attitude—with the help of the teaching about individual retribution—towards all doubts about its dogma, betrays its inability to win free from the prophetic tension between the divine Ought and the life in creation.

Thus the contradiction between the actual state of the world and the divine intention of the Creator is indelibly impressed in Old Testament thought, and cannot be composed by means of any temporary solution. Rather, man sees himself pressed to the limit of his earthly existence by the divine demand, and directed towards a new order whose only assurance lies in the promise of God.

3. *Hindrances arising from evil in the world*

This view was given depth and strength by the experience of manifold misfortunes and threats to existence. For the more

[41] Cf. especially the speeches of the friends in Job and the significance of the belief in retribution found in many Psalms (37, 39, 49, 73, 128) and in Prov. 1.19, 31ff.; 2.21f.; 3.33f., etc. See also p. 59ff.

[42] Job 38-42 (cf. p. 61); Eccl. 3.16ff.; 4.1ff.; 7.15; 8.10, and the criticism of supposed wisdom in 1.17f.; 3.11; 7.14, 23f.; 8.17.

D*

conscious man became of his destiny as bearer of God's will in the world of creation, the more vivid was the question in his mind concerning the evils in the world which opposed this destiny. A hasty glance at the Old Testament witnesses might lead one to suppose that this question never arose during the period of unbroken national power. All one can hear are the utterances of the dominant mood of joy in life. In this mood the people confidently proceeds to carry out the task which has been set it, and makes light of the many hardships and cruelties of the world as the inevitable accompaniment of a state of affairs which must be submitted to as divinely ordained.[43] The predominantly collective sense of life in ancient Israel makes it easy to understand the strength of the resistance shown by the individual to the powers which threatened his life. Where the individual life was so inextricably bound up with the whole life of the people that it could see no possibility of existing outside the people and the tribe, then the personal affairs of the individual were bound to be secondary to the dominant interest in the fortunes of the whole people. All claims upon life and happiness could be silenced by the one great care and joy which filled all life—the prosperity and happiness of the whole. Only when this was threatened could the meaning of life become ambiguous,[44] and certainty about God be afflicted by the doubt whether he had abandoned his people.[45]

If the individual, in face of heavy afflictions, was able to take refuge in this way in the collective sense of life with its own interpretation of misfortune, it must at the same time be recognized that even in early times voices were raised in Israel which

[43] Cf., for instance, the characteristic utterance of Joab, the captain of the host, in II Sam. 10.1, or David's words after grievous losses in war, in II Sam. 11.25. Cf. similar words from very late times, in Esth. 4.16f.

[44] I Sam. 4.20f.

[45] Cf. especially the national laments in the Psalter, as Ps. 74, 79, 80, which were sung to the community on fast-days and at mourning festivals, and which—though in their present form perhaps of a later date—derive from a primitive *genre*.

betray a deep sense of the toil and trouble, the need and the curse with which human life is afflicted. In the parenthetical remark of the wise woman of Tekoah to David, in which may be heard a passionate complaint about the quick passing of life —'For we must needs die, and are as water spilt on the ground'[46]—we may perceive an undercurrent in the Israelite view of life, in which the contradiction between the divine goal of life and the presence of uncomprehended suffering keeps thought in tormented tension. And the comprehensive judgement on the labour and sorrow of men in Gen. 3, groaning beneath the curse which burdens the world and the soil, depicts in all its severity the grim fate of death as the end of all human hope and longing. This judgement gives us an inkling of the range of the temptation provided by the constant threat to human happiness. This temptation remained as a living part of Israel's whole history, as we may see, for instance, in that melancholy retrospective glance of the patriarch Jacob, 'Few and evil have the days of the years of my life been',[47] and no less in the poetic description of the frailty of human life, like grass or the flower of the field in its transient glory,[48] or in Job's moving complaint about the wearisome hireling labour which is mortal man's appointed fate.[49]

The temptation which the suffering in life brings, and which is similarly expressed in the laments of Babylon and Egypt, is particularly grave for Israel, as even in the most bitter events it has to do with no other power save that same God whose call gives life its meaning and its goal. As in the revelation of the Covenant he shows himself to be the limitless Giver, so on the other hand he shows himself as the One who incomprehensibly deprives and rejects. With other peoples the world of demons or the magic arts of evil men can be held responsible for sudden

[46] II Sam. 14.14.
[47] Gen. 47.9:P.
[48] Ps. 103.14-16; Isa. 40.6f.; cf. Ps. 78.39; 89.48f.; Ecclus. 18.7f.; Job 14.1f.
[49] Job 7.1ff.

misfortune, and thus the good will of the gods can be separated from a world of curses which has its own laws and must be combated by opposing magic and exorcism. In Israel the responsibility of the contradiction between blessing and threat to life falls upon the God who has called man to serve him and jealously watches that no other power is allowed to influence the life of his community. That is why something of the uncanny and the demonic enters into the portrayal of his power.[50] But the astonishing thing is that his Being is not tainted by any devilish features: the malicious hatred and envy which disfigure the picture of the Babylonian and Greek gods are quite foreign to his Being. Even in the presence of inexplicable tribulations there is a readiness to acknowledge his higher justice, without any sceptical despair, such as we find in Babylon,[51] in his fundamental will to save. The communication of life which Israel experienced in the covenantal relations proves stronger than the temptation presented by the suffering of life.

This does not prevent a lively sense of the contradiction between suffering and death, and man's divinely ordained position of privilege in the whole of creation. This contradiction, in fact, gradually becomes a heavy burden on the whole feeling for life. The ever new attempts to master this contradiction, with the help of the living experience of God, have largely contributed to the characteristic quality of the Old Testament understanding of existence.

Without trying to outline the whole extent of this struggle —which would be beyond the scope of this study—we may take two specially vivid and significant moments: first, the early strong effort to pass beyond a purely negative evaluation of evil, as what ought not to be, to an acknowledgement and satisfactory setting of this disturbing fact in the total view of

---

[50] Cf. Gen. 32.25ff.; Ex. 4.24ff.

[51] Cf. the 'Geschichte eines Leidenden und seine Erlösung' in *Altorientalische Texte zum Alten Testament*, ed. H. Gressmann, 2nd ed. 1926, p. 275.

human destiny; and secondly, the inflexible concern with the truth, which did not permit a harmonizing of incompatibles, but on the very basis of the increasingly rich and profound knowledge of God compelled Israel to pause before the inexplicable fact of suffering.

Basic to this struggle with the problem of evil, in Israel as elsewhere, was first the fact that the origin of suffering was held to be the displeasure and wrath of the Deity, a view whose truth was taken for granted by every religion, and second the fact that this divine wrath was held to be due to the trespass of men. A new element, however, was present from the beginning in the experience of the God of the Covenant, who by proclaiming his will emerged from the sphere of arbitrary self-will characteristic of the heathen gods, and set the whole of life in the order of his clear laws. Here God's wrath was bound to be expressed chiefly in righteous retribution, which was the consequence of the violation of well-known laws; and it is this element of retribution which brought evil within the scheme of God's lordship over his people. Far from being only a cruel and meaningless fate, misfortune—first of the people and then secondarily of the individual—was given meaning as a valuable, indeed an indispensable means of protecting God's Covenant from deliberate disturbance and damage. In fact it was even possible to see in the sending of evil God's saving will, warning the guilty man and calling him to turn while there is time, before he is snatched away by the judgement of destruction.[52] Following this line of thought, education and purification became more and more clearly visible as the purpose of suffering. The story of Joseph, with its fine account of the well-thought-out punishment of the brothers, shows a deep understanding of the educative value of punishment. But it was the prophets who again and again tried to impress on their people that God's true love and patience are shown in the chain of afflictions in the

[52] Cf., for example, Gen. 20 and Josh. 7.

past which aimed at keeping open for the wanderers the way home to their Father's house. The Wisdom literature brought this thought to full power by explaining the suffering of the individual as the fatherly chastisement of the divine Master, which as a healing medicine actually indicated the divine favour.[53]

There is no doubt that on this line of thought the contradiction between suffering and the divine goal of human life could in large measure be smoothed away. This was all the more possible since there was joined to this way of thinking a deep sense of the decisive power of sin over human life—a consequence of the prophetic preaching which was having a marked effect on the thought of the whole nation.[54] And yet the light cast on the problem of suffering at this point was bound to deepen and intensify its enigmatic quality in another direction—namely, in the suffering of the innocent and the doubt thus cast on God's righteous retribution. The more vivid the faith in God as the incorruptible Judge, the more incomprehensible his silence in face of the ill-fortune and defeat of the righteous and the triumph of the godless. The earlier period, alert to the mysterious and wonderful rule of the great and inscrutable God, and ready to subordinate the individual to the whole, was still able to suppress, or to keep out of the forefront of its consciousness, the questions which were waiting here. They were bound to break out all the more violently when people and State, under the misrule of blinded princes and a corrupt ruling class, drove on to destruction, and the individual, summoned to personal responsibility, saw himself delivered to a terrible fate in atoning for the guilt of his fathers. In the bitter words, 'The fathers have eaten sour grapes, and the children's teeth are set on edge', whose wide distribution is

[53] Prov. 3.12; Job 36.5ff.; taken up into the confession of the righteous in Ps. 66.10; 118.18; 119.67, 71; Lam. 3.27.

[54] Cf. p. 67f. Yet the old Israelite writer in Gen. 3 and the following passages of primitive history was able to depict impressively the close connexion of suffering and death with man's guilty estrangement from God.

attested by the double transmission in the Old Testament,[55] the solidarity of connexion with the whole nation and with earlier generations is rejected as an intolerable assault upon life, condemning it to despair. There arose a most insistent demand for a new attitude to the problem of evil which might give assurance to the individual about the goal of his life.

In the intellectual struggle which began round this point, the temptation to master the tormenting problem by means of a theodicy became acute for the first time. Undoubtedly the rational element in the Israelite belief in God furnished certain preconditions for the effort to bring the happenings of the world into a reasoned system, by whose help they could be understood as the purposeful order of a good and righteous God. The ancient Eastern belief in the gods was inadequate to this task : the conflict of divine powers ran contrary to any comprehensive unity, and permitted in the end only the conception of a universal law, which in the form of impersonal fate forced life under its power. For Greek thought, on the other hand, exercised by the same question, the effort to attain to a theodicy was congenial to its nature, since with its tendency to see the cosmos as a unity it was bound to feel distressed by the natural and moral evils in the world as by a disturbing element, and to press towards a harmonious settlement. Thus the Platonic-Stoic view of the world attributed special importance to this very theme of a theodicy in its teaching about divine providence, and as an essential part of its system it constructed the proof of a perfect world order, in which God's planned government of the world was reconciled with its present imperfection.

This smooth dovetailing of the problem into the total view of the world and of man was not possible in Israel. But characteristically there was the strongest resistance to any such attempt, during which it became clearer and clearer that in the fact of evil in the world there was a hindrance to belief in a righteous

[55] Jer. 31.29; Ezek. 18.2.

sovereign God which could not be overcome by a rational solution of the difficulties. The attempt could indeed be made to apply to the fate of the individual the old belief in retribution, which spoke of the happiness of the righteous and the misery of the godless, and thereby to prove that in every single instance those faithful to the Law received an earthly reward and those who were unfaithful were punished. This attempt to give meaning to the present, as the scene where righteous divine government of the world is carried out, could also be supported by proving that the same principles held good without exception in the past, as is attempted, for instance, in the interpretation of history given in the Book of Chronicles. This energetic effort to explain the world in a clear scheme, and to rescue the doctrine of divine righteousness as an irrefragable principle of reason,[56] could, it is true, set at rest many doubts; it could render many contradictions in hard reality more tolerable, with the help of the idea of testing and educating, or of the final reckoning, or of the blessing in store for one's children. But it failed at the very point where it should really have proved itself—that of the inexplicable evil fortune of the righteous. Where it was obstinately maintained, it involved in the last resort the unjust branding of every unfortunate man as guilty. In order to save God's honour it therefore led to the denial of the simple truth, to the most poisonous transformation of piety into hypocrisy.

But it was not only as a consequence of this assault upon the suffering righteous man that opposition arose to the abstract theoretical elaboration of the belief in retribution, even though it is true that the trial endured by Job by the heartless condemnation on the part of his former friends gives passion to his lamentations. It is rather the recognition that such a schematization of the divine rule involves a fundamental misunderstanding of the Being of the true God, and is the real attack upon his

[56] Wisdom teachers (cf. Prov. 1.19, 31ff.; 2.21f.; 3.31ff., etc.) as well as the Psalmist (cf. Ps. 3.7; 39; 49; 73; 128) have attempted this.

honour. This recognition leads to a protest against the rigid mechanism of the scheme, and encourages the struggle for a new understanding of divine action. In this as in every attempt to construct a theodicy the residual mystery of the divine majesty was forgotten, and the limitless freedom of the divine action was dragged into the light of human comprehension, which exalted itself as judge over the incomprehensible ways of divine governance, confining them within the narrow categories of reward and punishment. There was no trace left of silence before the enigma of the inscrutable divine self-sufficiency, of trembling before the uncanny and overpowering divine sovereignty, of the humbling and at the same time exalting awareness of an infinitely superior creative Wisdom such as had given even the early faith of Israel its unpretentiousness, its sense of awe, and its powerful range. God had rather become a demon, only watching man in order to be able, like a ruthless inquisitor, to drag him to justice, and to revel in the tortures of the wretched, as Job 7.11ff. and 10.13ff. plainly depict him. In the speeches of God in the Book of Job this God of men's construction is opposed to the incomprehensibly wonderful Creator God, who cannot be caught in a system of reasonable purposes, but escapes all human calculation.[57] If his greatness nevertheless does not simply oppress and destroy man, but calls him to adoration and admiration, the reason lies in the deep inner solidarity of connexion between the creature and his Creator, which summons man, as the one who can be addressed by the divine Word, to personal community with the hidden Lord of the world, and opens his mind to what is simply precious and wonderful in the divine rule, even when he does not understand it. In thus convincing the human spirit which is open to him of his higher right, he who reigns in mystery frees man from the torment of his pain-filled questions, and nullifies man's desire for a rational and comprehensible world order. It is just through uncompre-

[57] Job 38-42.

hended suffering that positive appreciation of the inscrutable possibilities and glories of God's richness as Creator can become a free act of willing surrender. In this act man acknowledges his divine destiny, despite all the contradictions presented by the world, even if he waits before God's door all his life.

Thus the Old Testament belief in the Creator, which speaks not of a first cause but of the absolute source of this world, was unfolded here in all its grandeur; it was protected from a solution which was rational in the sense of being explained by a world reason enmeshed in purpose. At the same time a second attack on the dogma of individual retribution, teaching a new application of the prophetic message, freed faith from a dangerous threat to its certainty about God. When inexplicable misfortune is understood as a sign of hidden guilt, as is urged by the logical doctrine of retribution,[58] then the individual's relation to God can always be attacked and questioned as an illusion. On the other hand the undisturbed happiness of those who scorn God must awaken suspicion and mistrust of God's action in the heart of the sufferer, since such happiness is not in accord with the supreme norm of righteousness. Here the believer saw himself faced with deciding whether he should attribute more importance to outward good fortune or evil fortune than to the experience of steadfast loyalty and refreshing richness of life which came from intercourse with the living God, and with the Word of his grace. The prophets considered that the faith which ignored all external hostile powers and turned to the invisible divine power, clinging to his word of promise, had the true grasp of reality. So, when the individual's life was threatened by hard blows of fate, it had to be proved whether in faith there is access to a reality in which outward good fortune or evil fortune lose their significance and can no longer prevent life being filled with meaning. In Jeremiah's

[58] The strong hold this view had on the Jews may be seen from the question the disciples addressed to Jesus concerning the man born blind, John 9.2.

struggle this conquest of suffering by a deliberate turning to the divine source of life takes visible form for the first time. As he had to endure in his own body the agonizing question of a theodicy,[59] he was able to bear witness in his confessions to the higher reality which is revealed to faith.[60] What Jeremiah went through in his own experience, as one called to special service, it was the aim of the writer of the Book of Job to express for all who were perplexed by the same question, in his picture of the great sufferer. In Job's dialogue with his friends he represents in masterly fashion the gradual escape of the suffering righteous man, under the pressure of temptation, from setting too high a value on outward circumstances. The decisive question for Job's life, in the light of which the riddle of suffering and of righteous retribution loses its significance, is whether the God who in other respects remembered his worshipper and forgave sin, who as Creator could not abandon his work and as a righteous God must help the oppressed to obtain justice,[61] would speak a gracious and positive word to his life and suffering. And the assurance that not even death, which otherwise pitilessly destroys every connexion with God, can prevent the divine Lord coming to the help of his servant, leads Job finally, in defiance of all human reproaches and accusations, to the triumphant issue at the end of the disputation. In the Word of justification spoken by God which Job confidently awaits, he finds a completely satisfactory substitute for the external confirmation of God's good pleasure in the enjoyment of the goods of life. For here, even in the face of death, life in the fullest sense is disclosed, such as is present only where God calls man to himself.[62]

[59] Jer. 12.1-6.
[60] Jer. 15.15-21; 17.9ff.
[61] Job 7.8, 20f.; 10.8-12; 14.7ff., 15; 13.9ff.; 16.18-17.9; 23.7.
[62] We agree with Sellin, *Das Problem des Hiobbuches*, 1919, in seeing this as the purpose of the dialogue in Job, ch. 3-31, whose original intention was, however, later disturbed and diverted by new settings of the problem.

What in Job is a painful struggle towards the light is clear and full in the witness of the writers of the Psalms, who joyously lay hold of the self-disclosure of the great God for spiritual community with his faithful people as the incomparable treasure which gives meaning to even an outwardly unsuccessful life. In the audacious image which describes God as his portion, the writer of the 73rd Psalm summarizes what gives life an unfading value, even if it knows nothing of rich enjoyments and pleasant days, and even if it has to meet an untimely end. For this portion remains, even when body and soul disappear in death. When God upholds and guides and removes, the believer finds his ultimate shelter here, even if he can say nothing about the way in which God will maintain his connexion with him—for here all earthly imaginings fall short. So too there is disclosed to the poet of Psalm 16, in living intercourse with God, who gives the succour of his presence to his people, advising and guiding them, an inward happiness which far surpasses all outward goods and cannot be touched by the grave or the world of the dead. Here the Psalmist sees a 'path of life' revealed to him (verse 11), which will lead him in the end beyond all barriers of earthly life to 'fulness of joy', springing from full and untroubled community with his God.

It is therefore the question of God which both here and in similar passages[63] takes the place of the question of suffering, and indicates the only significant life, which needs no support from a theodicy. It is not that the contradictions in the present state of the world are thereby resolved or even deprived of their power. In the triumphant witness of faith there is a clear 'nevertheless', which has not overcome the adversary, but is certain that it will compel him to yield again and again. A false harmonizing of the contradictions in the world is here, too, replaced by the connexion with a reality superior

[63] Cf. Ps. 17.15; 63.4.

to the course of the world, which cannot be theoretically proved but is grasped only where there is thinking in a new dimension.

A third attack on the attempt to make a theodicy, however, strikes at the root of the tension between the world's need and God's promise with its threat to individual existence. This opposes to the whole of present life a new world of God which is already breaking in, and conceives of earthly existence as a service for this coming world. The source of the strength of the theory of individual retribution, which by a kind of inner necessity was continually asserting itself, was that this tense expectation which filled the prophetic period of a change-over into a new aeon had yielded to a modest sense of the earthly imperfections of the divine community. Hence the struggle to establish an order of Law, as the great goal of the people's history, was at the centre of religious thought. In this struggle, which was made more difficult by the strife of parties within the community and by the oppression of pagan overlords, the strength to endure rested upon the firm confidence that God with his righteous retribution would finally bring all human resistance to naught. Hence the proof of this retribution in the life of every member of the community was of central significance for belief in God's government of the world. In the just distribution of blessings and evils seemed to lie the only clear comprehension of God's living presence, and the guarantee both of the content and of the ultimate triumph of the community.

These postulates lose their power only where it is recognized as an illegitimate human anticipation of the divine purpose with the world to make the righteous community absolute, instead of treating it as a modest interim community whose destiny is to give way to a new world order filled with the glory of the divine creator. Here the view is to the future. Present good or ill fortune are deprived of their exaggerated significance as a testing of God, by means of which God has to justify his ways to men. But one must follow the Lord of the world, who is leading all things to the great turning-point into the new aeon, in order to be used in his service in full and faithful trust. In this way there arises a new relation of innocent human suffering to God's action. As vicarious suffering it fits into the divine decree of the reconciliation and salvation of the ungodly. In his Songs of the Servant of God[64] the anonymous prophet of the Exile proclaims the mystery of representative action as the inmost vocation of the Saviour chosen by God, who by his suffering creates a new people of God. The unique service of this Messianic figure is seen to consist in showing the individual the way in which he must regard his personal sufferings.[65] Then from this new interpretation of God's action for the fulfilment of his kingdom it comes to be understood that the suffering imposed by God does not mean that one is outcast from his love, but on the contrary that one is taken up into his service and honoured by a specially important task. It is true that in Deutero-Zechariah the service of the good shepherd is ascribed to a unique saving figure.[66] But at the same time the individual begins to realize that the same charge is laid upon his own life. Whether the sufferer in Psalm 22, absorbed with the pains of death, experiences his affliction as a part or an anticipation of the fate which the suffering righteous man must one day undergo, in order that the whole history of Israel might reach its goal, the victory of the kingdom of God in the whole world;[67] or whether the Psalmist in Psalm 118 understands his course through death and destruction as a divine chastisement[68] by means of which the divine plan for the world takes a decisive step towards the saving consummation[69]—in both instances suffering is seen in the light of eschatological fulfilment; it is understood as the most effective means by which God sets up his lordship over humanity. It is in suffering that the afflicted

[64] Isa. 42.1-8; 49.1-6; 50.4-9; 52.13-53.12.
[65] Isa. 50.10.
[66] Zech. 11.4-13.1.

[67] Ps. 22.28f.
[68] Ps. 118.18, 21.
[69] Ps. 118.22, 23.

man is nearest to God, and that the painful calculation of the scheme of retribution is brought *ad absurdum*. The way of the cross becomes the true straight way to glory, the way by which the honour remains with God alone.

This glory includes the conquest of death as the last threat to the divine community. With an inner logic the conviction about the irreplaceable service of suffering in the establishment of God's kingship moves on to the saying about the destruction of death (Isa. 25.8), whose unlimited dominion in the present calls God's plan for the world in question (Isa. 26.18). The break-through of the divine revelation of glory brings God's community with his people to perfection : for he not only recalls to life and to a share in his victory those who have gone to death for his cause,[70] but he 'overthrows the land of shades' (Isa. 26.19), and thus brings to triumph the whole of life throughout his creation. Thus the individual's assurance of faith in face of the threat of death is taken up into the total view of the divine action which is leading to a new creation.

It is clear that this does not mean that a new theory about the meaning of suffering has been established, which might be illuminating for everyone. For this positive attitude to suffering is a completely free personal act which is possible only as the venture of a faith to which the coming world of God is more certain than the trivial reality of everyday, with its oppression and its hopelessness. As in the triumphant establishment of faith in the Creator, and of the experience of God's immediate nearness, so here there is the awakening of a wholly new readiness to take the authoritative presence of God seriously—a presence to whose hidden depths suffering also belongs—and to renounce every theory which does not come within reach of the divine richness. Here one can certainly no longer be self-assured in the possession and disposal of one's life; but one

[70] Dan. 12.1-3; Ps. 22.28-31.

must simply stand and wait, in that human existence which one knows to be provisional, surrounded and upheld by the eternity of God.

4. *Hindrances arising from wickedness*

In the same way, finally, the severest shock which threatens man's understanding of existence on the basis of unconditioned Ought—namely, the question raised by the fact of wickedness —is suffered in all its unmitigated strength. It is true that the will of the divine election is also revealed as a will to forgiveness, which in spite of the people's sinful disloyalty holds fast to the Covenant, and provides the assurance that the conquest of wickedness is included in God's plan of salvation. The God of the Covenant shows himself as a merciful and gracious God, long-suffering and abundant in goodness and truth, when he interprets to Moses the mystery hidden in his name.[71] Thus the intercessions of the leaders he has commissioned can again and again be interposed in full confidence between the sinful people and the threat of the divine wrathful judgement, and can plead for the overcoming of wickedness by means of forgiveness.[72] In the expiatory offering God himself has provided a means of forgiveness, by which man witnesses to his repentance and submission to the divine verdict, relying upon God's will to forgive.[73]

But this does not prevent man's existence being imperilled by God's judgement. The Covenant as such never works as an automatic insurance against the punishment which threatens the sinner, but joined to it is the curse of the Covenant which

[71] Ex. 34.6.
[72] Gen. 18.23ff.; 20.7; Ex. 32.11-14, 32; 34.8f.; Num. 14.13-19; I Sam. 7.8f.; 12.19, 23; 15.11; Amos 7.1-6; Jer. 15.11; 37.3; 42.2; Ezek. 13.5; 22.30.
[73] II Sam. 24.17ff.; Job 42.8f.; Lev. 4 and 5.

forecasts the destruction of him who breaks the Covenant.[74] It follows, then, that God's intervention and punishment must again and again be experienced in fear and trembling for the existence of the people of the Covenant.[75] Even where praise of God's unshakable faithfulness reaches such a height that it dares to speak of his Covenant lasting for ever,[76] terrible divine punishments are not excluded. This peril engendered by wickedness, which is a constant source of fear, reaches its climax in the preaching of the prophets, which proclaims the complete destruction of Israel as a punishment for its breach of the Covenant, and which weighs on the whole present state of the world as a serious threat which makes life meaningless. For it holds out the certain prospect of God's final break with the people of his choice, and thus with the universal story of salvation with its large horizons and rich hopes.

Now it is true that other nations have also known moods in which the end of the world loomed. In Babylon and in Egypt prophecies were current of coming catastrophes of the most terrible nature, which would bring to an end the present world order and sweep everything to appalling destruction.[77] These expectations were taken over by the Greeks and were expressed in the teaching of the ages of the world and of the great year of the worlds,[78] as well as in ecstatic mass movements. But since, in spite of profound moral and religious conceptions, the development of the world on the Greek view is dominated by dispensations of fate, *fatum*, these expectations were never able to exercise any decisive influence on the Greek spirit. It was

---

[74] Ex. 32.10; Deut. 27. 15ff.; 28.15ff.; Lev. 26.14ff.

[75] Ex. 32.25ff.; Num. 25 1ff.; Josh. 7; Judg. 20f.; I Sam. 15.7ff.; I Kings 19.15ff.

[76] Judg. 2.1; Gen. 9.16; 17.7, etc.

[77] Cf. *Altorientalische Texte zum Alten Testament*, ed. H. Gressmann, 2nd ed., pp. 46ff., 212ff., 283f.; also O. Weber, *Die Literatur der Babylonier und Assyrer*, 1907, pp. 104ff.

[78] Hesiod, *Works and Days*, 109ff.

different with Israel. Here the announcement of the coming destruction was not a Cassandra call, born of a sense of impending revolutions, or the cosmic teaching of priestly wisdom, but a message from the same God whose summons and rule gave meaning and content to life. The reason given for this impending destruction can be linked with that lively threat to the Covenant which was felt from the beginning, and provides a persuasive total interpretation of history. For what was felt in ancient times to be an isolated invasion of evil into the world as ordained by God, which could be dealt with in good time by watchfulness and care, was now given coherence and depth by the prophets' preaching, and disclosed as the uncanny power of fundamental hostility to God. For the prophets' interpretation of God's action with his people, as love which woos them and fatherly faithfulness which sustains them, raises the relation with God above the legal fulfilment of commandments, and transfers it to confident surrender in faith, love and obedience. A breach of the Covenant can therefore no longer be understood as a violation of individual ordinances which can be put right again, even if by heavy sacrifices. Rather, its essence is revealed as a deliberate turning away of man from his God, which leads to inner estrangement and to the total destruction of the faithfulness which is reflected in the pictures of marriage and betrothal, of the place of a son and the duty of the vassal. So the whole strength and grandeur of this inner change is illuminated: its demonic spell permits none who have come under it any hope of return, its rampant canker spares no order or class of society and irremediably corrupts the whole history of the nation, leaving death as the only way of escape. Every moralistic weakening of sin as an isolated deviation from the norm is made impossible. What happens is that the destiny of human life and being takes a false direction, in which every member of the nation without exception is involved.

The prophets are also able to speak in new ways of God's will to forgive. They proclaim the God who brings upon the sinner the utmost severity of his judgement precisely in order that he may open the way to a new fellowship with himself.[79] He causes his forgiving grace to dawn upon those who have been spoiled of all earthly goods and are ripe for humility.[80] Those who appear in the eyes of the whole world as heavily punished and abandoned to destruction, such as those who were driven into exile, will experience the miracle of forgiveness by which they are destined to new life.[81] Thus in the midst of judgement appears a new possibility of life, which is offered by God. This has nothing to do with human calculations, nor is it substantiated by the restoration of the lost national glory. But it is possessed by a faith which reaches boldly out beyond all the darkness of the present. Lastly, this affirmation of the divine gift of grace, despite all appearances, is also at the very heart of the priestly handling of the Law, in so far as that had to win its way against the pressure of political helplessness and dependence on heathen nations. Although no proof of the divine pleasure, in the form of a restoration of external good fortune, was given to this priestly work, yet God's forgiving action can be called to witness as a reality, which proves its power within the framework of a community firmly integrated in cultic and in social forms.

But in face of a world of sin and injustice, whose baneful effects are to be seen even in the circle of the faithful, and the reality of whose temptation is seen in the bitter complaints of the Psalms about the oppression of the righteous by the wicked, the way indicated here can only be a way of ' nevertheless '. For it cannot be separated from a humble acknowledgement to God the Judge that man is lost without excuse. It demands unconditional submission to what God in his freedom ordains, even if he is gracious. So this way can only be gone by him who is ready to yield his own right of existence utterly, with its claims

---

[79] Isa. 6.5-7; 28.16ff.; 30.15.
[80] Zeph. 3.2, 11f.
[81] Isa. 49-55; Jer. 29.12-14; Ezek. 18; 33.10f.

E

and its reservations. It is no wonder that there is no end to the efforts made, under various guises, to soften this hard way, and to mitigate the radical judgement on the present state of affairs.

One form of this effort is seen in the setting of the riddle of evil in a general system of law by connecting it with man's earthly finitude and creaturely weakness.[82] This lifts the sinful course of human life out of the sphere of responsible action, and makes it approximate to a natural state calculated to evoke rather the pity of the Creator for his weak creature than the wrath of the Judge.[83] The danger behind this effort is that one drifts into a pessimistic judgement of creation and of the whole area in which creation is active. This would call in question the essential Israelite declaration of faith in the Creator. This faith provides, indeed, the most powerful hindrance to a logical evaluation of the possibility of escaping the threat of radical evil. That is why other witnesses give an opposite interpretation to those we have quoted, and see in the wretched human lot the consequence of God's righteous wrath punishing man's rebellion.[84]

Expiation by means of the cult seems to offer another way out for human guilt. It is true that the naïve confidence that guilt can be as it were bought off by a substantial sacrifice to God, was dealt a mortal blow by the prophets' destructive criticism of such pious business arrangements. Even the priestly code, by giving prominence to the fact that God himself provides the means of expiation, prevents the misunderstanding that a self-effective human action is being carried out. It gives the expiation offered in the cult a personal character as the means of forgiveness in which God testifies to his saving will. But when the expiatory effect is extended to all sacrifice, the need arises for a stronger manifestation of divine forgiveness. The extensive elaborations and supplements to the priestly code are

[82] Job 4.17-21; 7.1ff.; 14.1-6.
[83] Job 7.7-10, 17-21; Ps. 103.13-16; 78.38f.; 89.47-49; 144.3f.
[84] Ps. 90.5-9; Isa. 40.6ff.

an indication of the effort made to extend and to complete the priestly system of rites of expiation.[85] This betrays the dangerous inclination to strengthen the guaranteed effect of the act of expiation by an increase in the number and size of the rites, at the expense of the really important thing—the divine promise and pledge. Here the cult readily assumes the character of a great apparatus of expiation, to which the faithful cling for protection from the corrupting power of evil, more than to the divine assurance of full forgiveness and a new creation of God's people and each of its members.

It is all the more important that the divine sovereign prerogative of forgiveness, which is not bound or limited to any sacrificial system, should again and again find living witnesses. In Psalms such as 40, 51 and 69 the assurance of pardon as the immediate gift of God is opposed to every attempt to ascribe a monopoly in forgiveness to the expiatory rites. The complete dependence of sinful man on the free compassion of God, which cannot be guaranteed by any earthly act, is once again firmly maintained.

The most powerful influence of all is exercised by a third way of escape from the heavy pressure of radical guilt—by taking refuge in human achievement as the means of establishing a holy community. Piety which is oriented towards the Law is always inclined, in defending individual failure and fulfilling individual commandments, to overlook the deep roots and unbreakable bonds of active sin in the human will, and thus to put great trust in obedience to the Law. This inclination is the stronger in proportion to the resoluteness with which the ideal of the holy community, which is to be realized with the help

---

[85] The most striking instance of these efforts is the elaboration of the Festival of the great Day of Atonement (Lev. 16) by the joining together of originally separate rites and actions in one impressive whole. The sketch of the cult in the appendix to Ezekiel (cc. 43-46), in which the effort to obtain security from future sin leads to a remarkable recasting of the divine service, is also a part of this effort.

of the Law, is grasped by the pious and understood as the divine goal of the world. Here the affliction of bondage to sin no longer appears hopeless. The Law is the cure, which makes it possible for man by free choice to take the side of the good, and even to acquire merits which give him a claim on God's good pleasure. The free gift of divine grace disappears more and more behind an impartial retribution, which rewards the blameless fulfilment of the Law, and acknowledges the expiatory offerings made in works of love, in the study of the Torah and in almsgiving as of equal value with sacrifice. Here a ready confession of human sinfulness can no longer lead to an utter surrender to the grace of God. The habit grows of regarding sinfulness as a weakness which can gradually be overcome, for which satisfaction can be rendered to the divine righteousness by all kinds of expiation. Even sinlessness, which was imputed to the great righteous men of the past, becomes a goal also to be attained in the present: one day of blameless fulfilment of the Law will bring about the coming of the Messiah and his reign over the world.

This effort, which was intended to lead, despite all obstacles, to the mastery of life's problems, was made with astonishing energy. With proud confidence the man versed in the Law looked upon the clear lines of his own life and felt that in the possession of the true wisdom he was far superior to the fools and the godless.[86] But here too the attempt failed to master the constant threat to existence which comes from the prophetic view of sin. The attempt to lighten the burden of guilt was balanced by the uncertainty which is necessarily found in all human calculations. How is the doubt to be allayed whether the actual achievements satisfy the inexorable divine justice, when moral obligation falls apart into countless external regulations? Action is bound to be dominated by anxious formal service, turning the Law into a slave-driver which deprives

[86] Ps. 119.98ff.; Job 32.8ff.; Prov. 8.1ff.; Sol. 8.10ff.; 9.16ff.

moral action of all joy. From the time when the prophetic writings were accepted as part of the canon, the prophets' proclamation of the incorruptible Judge is heard again and again in Israel. It could not be silenced by the distinction between mortal and venial sins, or by an emphasis on particularly meritorious actions and works of love. The individual's certainty of salvation suffered great distress. The overweening assurance of the men of the Law easily changed, in natures of any depth, into helplessness and despair, as happened in the end in 4 Ezra and in Saul the Pharisee.

In one way or the other, then, the attempt to cover over the gnawing sense of guilt fails in what it sets out to do. The man who is held fast in the realm of the Ought is at the mercy of the knowledge that the power of evil sets an inescapable riddle before him, which he is unable to solve in his own strength. Once again, but now in a decisive and final way, he sees that he is banned from the self-contained circle of a harmonious interpretation of the world. Now he must surrender all desire to be at home in earthly circumstances and to have his roots there, because it is opposed to knowledge of the truth which has come to him. He resolutely abandons all hopeless human striving, and turns to the God who to the word of judgement adds the word of forgiveness, loosening the bond of guilt and disclosing a new life. At the same time he is fully aware that this forgiveness is a miracle of divine freedom which he cannot snatch as his due share, but which must rather be besought as an undeserved gift in humble patience and willing self-effacement. He who knocks on this door can make no claim, but yields his life into the hands of him who in ever fresh historical action acquits him and makes a new beginning possible. Thus to turn to God does not mean to flee from earthly reality to a realm of spiritual freedom where earthly laws have no power. But it means to take refuge with the absolute Lord of reality, who can give a new foothold to him who was lost and who in the midst of the hard laws of life provides a foretaste of the new divine world in which the power of evil is finally broken. For it is towards such a conclusive gift of reconciliation, in which the burden of sin in all its heaviness and extent and depth is lifted—finally and once for all lifted—that the patient expectation and prayers of the righteous are directed in their purest form.

This, then, is the response in the prayers of the community and of the individual to the prophetic proclamation of the judging and saving God; they point to the man who has come to see in forgiveness the succour without which all other goods are worthless.[87] Through all these prayers there runs the faithful waiting for the God who is known by his promises, though the soul waits 'more than they that watch for the morning', as in the classic words of Psalm 130. The centre of gravity of life is transferred from confident self-assertion in this earthly world to hoping for and expecting the coming God, whose saving act with sovereign power breaks through the ring of guilt and of the compulsion of sin, and discloses a new fellowship in which the riddle of evil is no more.

[87] Cf. Isa. 63.17; 64.5ff.; Ps. 51; 90; 130; Ezra 9.5ff.; Neh. 9; Dan. 9.4ff., 18f.

CHAPTER FOUR

LIFE UNDER THE PROMISE

T H E understanding of human existence from the basis of unconditional obligation leads, as we have shown in chapters one
and two, into a wide realm of life aiming at dominion over the
earth, yet having its firm centre in the shaping of the human
community on the basis of eternal norms. But where this circle
of life becomes a self-contained whole, then, as we tried to show
in chapter three, the realization of the great vision of the human
task is brought to a halt by the painful invasion of disturbing
powers, which arise from the incomprehensible confusion of
outer and inner development in man. Then the individual sees
himself thrust out into a merely makeshift existence, filled with
acute tensions. For every attempt to set the threatening facts
in order, and to make them into a part, perhaps a painful but
still an endurable part, of a completely balanced order of life
and of the universe, turns out to be impossible, since it involves
a denial of reality. The world in which and over which God's
power rules is not to be conceived as a closed system in which
man can take his assured place, and in fulfilling his destiny assert
his freedom and independence despite all disturbing powers. In
a world with the mark of death upon it, man's only resting-
point is in the Word of the God who as his Judge compels him
to condemn himself. It is the Word of promise which replaces
the old reality by a new reality which includes in a new creation
the individual as well as the people, the nations as well as the
whole of nature, and which resolves the insuperable resistance

to a life bound by an absolute obligation to God's will. In putting 'his law in their inward parts, and writing it in their hearts',[1] and in renewing the very heart of personal life by means of his spirit,[2] God establishes a community of will with his creatures which cannot be perfected in the present, and which has been the goal of his covenantal relation with Israel. In this way God creates the basic presuppositions for a new people in which the relation of the individual to the community accurately reflects his original will as Creator. The strength of renewal which streams out from this new action draws in the other peoples as well into a mighty process of transformation which brings a new humanity into God's service.[3] This turning-point in the world is completed in a cosmic renewal in virtue of which the whole creation returns to perfect beauty and harmony.[4]

The essential characteristic of this divine act of salvation, on which man in his need is cast back, is that it bears witness to a real entry of God into history. The questions arising in the community in its concrete earthly actuality are solved, they are not resolved into an enchanted fairy-tale unrelated to present need. The divine sovereign will which in the present gives human life its direction and destination, gives its stamp also to the world of the future. This appears most clearly in the figure of the Messianic Saviour-king. His earthly human appearance and his task as king of his people set the historical and moral renewal of the people and the world at the centre of the promised salvation—and this in spite of his having several super-human traits. But at the same time it is quite clear that no human earthly historical movement, whatever its form, is able to produce the new world of God as its natural fruit. As a supernatural divine reality the salvation of God must transform

---

[1] Jer. 31.33.   [2] Ezek. 36.26f.   [3] See Note 27, p. 36.
[4] Isa. 2.2; 11.6-9; 29.17; 32.15; Hos. 2.20, 23f.; Amos 9.11; Josh. 4.18; Zech. 14.6, 8, 10, etc. Cf. Gressmann, *Der Messias*, 1929, pp. 150ff., 164ff.

and re-create this world of violence and injustice. That is why, in describing this new reality, the language of myth, with its illuminating picture of the garden of paradise, appears on the scene quite of its own accord.

In this very union of historical reality with the supernatural glory of a divine re-creation, God's promise to man, who is held fast in the realm of the unconditional Ought, and yet suffers from the pressure of the contradictions which have broken out in this union, offers him the chance of affirming in practical life the will of God which has been revealed to him. He is offered the chance of letting this will take its effect as a real impulse, without his breaking under the strain. For the demand of the divine sovereign will to be a moral norm, which with its call to decision gives to life the character of a struggle, is in inward agreement with the expected and promised moral good of harmony between God and man. This confirms the promised fulfilment of life as giving meaning even to the earthly struggle and patchwork existence, a fulfilment grounded in the Being of the divine Lawgiver and Creator. As in the enigmas of history the realizing of the divine goal of the world is already on the way, so too human action, in spite of its broken and imperfect nature, becomes a witness to a perfect form of life which everyone who is called of God goes out to meet. What appeared first in the prophetic office as the most profound meaning of human action—serving as the unmistakable sign of the coming great revolution through God's power[5]—stands out more and more clearly as the task of the whole people and later of the individual as well. The great prophet of the exile calls on the Servant of God (whether he is identical with the people or appears as the Messianic Fulfiller[6]) as witness to God's saving righteousness in the course of world history. Just as Israel's greatest king, David,

---

[5] Isa. 8.18; 20.3; Hos. 1.2ff.; 3.1-5; Ezek. 12.11; 24.24, 27.
[6] Isa. 43.10, 12, 21; 44.8, 21 (read 'my witness' for 'my servant'); 48.6; 51.16. The same thought is fundamentally present in Ezekiel's view of Israel's relation to the nations, cf. Ezek. 5.5ff.; 36.20f.

found his honour in being God's witness to the nations,[7] so the function of the chosen people is to consist in the proper witness to God's glory. Just because it had gone through the deep night of separation from God, when suffering and guilt inextricably interwoven delivered it up to the accursed power of death, it is now able, when God's word of forgiveness calls it to life, to witness as none other can to the reality of God's world, which has already broken into this world and changed all its marks of death into marks of resurrection.

Thus for the individual, too, an all inclusive significance is given to the task which had been assigned to him from the beginning in the praise and service of God, as the messenger of salvation experienced in his own body.[8] He becomes aware that his whole life receives its real meaning as a witness to the world-transforming saving power of God at the very point where it breaks down outwardly and is renewed by God's promise.[9]

This narrow ridge runs between two dangers. On the one hand is the danger of betrayal of the divine 'Thou shalt' by haggling with its inexorability, in order to escape its severe judgement and to find a resting-place in the empirical present, where the fulfilment of existence can be anticipated. Here the forgiving long-suffering of God is regarded as the natural gift and saving institution of a sphere of life at rest in itself, and not as the wonder of wonders to be understood only on the basis of the coming final act of salvation. On the other hand there is the threat of a fanatical denial of the final questioning of the divine summons by the uncanny powers of destruction. For in arrogant self-confidence man thinks he can fulfil in his own strength the divine will which has been split into many individual commandments, and that he can thereby compel the agonizing tension to cease. Both dangers become acute where the dead authority of the formal law has replaced direct contact

[7] Isa. 55.4; cf. Ps. 89.26ff.
[8] Ps. 30.13; 32.6, 11; 34.4ff.; 40.10f.; 66.16ff.; 92.16; 116.13ff., etc.
[9] Ps. 22.28ff.; 51.16; 103.19ff.; 118.17, 22f.

with the will of God, which manifests itself as really present in demand and judgement, as well as in forgiveness and salvation. Thus in late Jewish times these dangers took actual shape, and in the parties of the Pharisees and the Sadducees as they struggled for the leadership they threatened the community with destruction. Between these two dangers runs the way of resolute affirmation of the provincial and patchwork nature of the present form of life, an affirmation which knows that it is supported by the divine grace which makes life possible. By the same grace the threat to human life is lifted and life is made worth living, for the first rays from the light of the coming salvation are already shining in its darkness.

INDEX OF BIBLICAL REFERENCES

Index of Biblical References

Index of Biblical References

Index of Biblical References